I0454797

BISHOP LAVAL

A. LEBLOND DE BRUMATH

[ZHINGOORA BOOKS]

This edition is published by
Zhingoora Books.

The Cover is Designed by Pallav Sethiya.

Apart from any fair dealing for the purposes of research or private study, or criti-cism or review, this publication may only be reproduced, stored or transmitted, in any form or by any means, with the prior permission in writing of the publishers. All disputes are subject to exclusive jurisdiction of Mandsaur Courts only. For any suggestions and feedback or book on new concept/domain, please contact us at the email given below.

zhingoora_books@yahoo.com

CONTENTS

CHAPTER I

ESTABLISHMENT OF THE CATHOLIC CHURCH IN CANADA

If, standing upon the threshold of the twentieth century, we cast a look behind us to note the road traversed, the victories gained by the great army of Christ, we discover everywhere marvels of abnegation and sacrifice; everywhere we see rising before us the dazzling figures of apostles, of doctors of the Church and of martyrs who arouse our admiration and command our respect. There is no epoch, no generation, even, which has not given to the Church its phalanx of heroes, its quota of deeds of devotion, whether they have become illustrious or have remained unknown.

Born barely three centuries ago, the Christianity of New France has enriched history with pages no less glorious than those in which are enshrined the lofty deeds of her elders. To the list, already long, of workers for the gospel she has added the names of the Récollets and of the Jesuits, of the Sulpicians and of the Oblate Fathers, who crossed the seas to plant the faith among the hordes of barbarians who inhabited the immense regions to-day known as the Dominion of Canada.

And what daring was necessary, in the early days of the colony, to plunge into the vast forests of North America! Incessant toil, sacrifice, pain and death in its most terrible forms were the price that was gladly paid in the service of God by men who turned their backs upon the comforts of civilized France to carry the faith into the unknown wilderness.

Think of what Canada was at the beginning of the seventeenth century! Instead of these fertile provinces, covered to-day by luxuriant harvests, man's gaze met everywhere only impenetrable forests in which the woodsman's axe had not yet permitted the plough to cleave and fertilize the soil; instead of our rich and populous cities, of our innumerable villages daintily perched on the brinks of streams, or rising here and there in the midst of verdant plains, the eye perceived only puny wigwams isolated and lost upon the banks of the great river, or perhaps a few agglomerations of smoky huts, such as Hochelaga or Stadaconé; instead of our iron rails, penetrating in all directions, instead of our peaceful fields over which trains hasten at marvellous speed from ocean to ocean, there were but narrow trails winding through a jungle of primeval trees, behind which hid in turn the Iroquois, the Huron or the Algonquin, awaiting the propitious moment to let fly the fatal arrow; instead of the numerous vessels bearing over the waves of the St. Lawrence, at a distance of more than six hundred leagues from the sea, the products of the five continents; instead of yonder floating palaces, thronged with travellers from the four corners of the earth, then only an occasional bark canoe came gliding slyly along by the reeds of the shore, scarcely stopping except to permit its crew to kindle a fire, to make prisoners or to scalp some enemy.

A heroic courage was necessary to undertake to carry the faith to these savage tribes. It was condemning one's self to lead a life like theirs, of ineffable hardships, dangers and privations, now in a bark canoe and paddle in hand, now on foot and bearing upon one's shoulders the things necessary for the holy sacrament; in the least case it was braving hunger and thirst, exposing one's self to the rigours of an excessive cold, with which European nations were not yet familiar; it often meant hastening to meet the most horrible tortures. In spite of all this, however, Father Le Caron did not hesitate to penetrate as far as the country of the Hurons, while Fathers Sagard and Viel were sowing the first seeds of Christianity in the St. Lawrence valley. The devotion of the Récollets, to the family of whom belonged these first missionaries of Canada, was but ill-rewarded, for, after the treaty of St. Germain-en-Laye, which restored Canada to France, the king refused them permission to return to a region which they had watered with the sweat of their brows and fertilized with their blood.

The humble children of St. Francis had already evangelized the Huron tribes as far as the Georgian Bay, when the Company of the Cent-Associés was founded by Richelieu. The obligation which the great cardinal imposed upon them of providing for the maintenance of the propagators of the gospel was to assure the future existence of the missions. The merit, however, which lay in the creation of a society which did so much for the furtherance of Roman Catholicism in North America is not due exclusively to the great cardinal, for Samuel de Champlain can claim a large share of it. "The welfare of a soul," said this pious founder of Quebec, "is more than the conquest of an empire, and kings should think of extending their rule in infidel countries only to assure therein the reign of Jesus Christ."

Think of the suffering endured, in order to save a soul, by men who for this sublime purpose renounced all that constitutes the charm of life! Not only did the Jesuits, in the early days of the colony, brave horrible dangers with invincible steadfastness, but they even consented to imitate the savages, to live their life, to learn their difficult idioms. Let us listen to this magnificent testimony of the Protestant historian Bancroft:—

"The horrors of a Canadian life in the wilderness were resisted by an invincible, passive courage, and a deep, internal tranquillity. Away from the amenities of life, away from the opportunities of vain-glory, they became dead to the world, and possessed their souls in unalterable peace. The few who lived to grow old, though bowed by the toils of a long mission, still kindled with the fervour of apostolic zeal. The history of their labours is connected with the origin of every celebrated town in the annals of French Canada; not a cape was turned nor a river entered but a Jesuit led the way."

Must we now recall the edifying deaths of the sons of Loyola, who brought the glad tidings of the gospel to the Hurons?—Father Jogues, who returned from the banks of the Niagara with a broken shoulder and mutilated hands, and went back, with sublime persistence, to his barbarous persecutors, to pluck from their midst the palm of martyrdom; Father Daniel, wounded by a spear while he was absolving the dying in the village of St. Joseph; Father Brébeuf, refusing to escape with the women and children of the hamlet of St. Louis, and expiring, together with Father Gabriel Lalemant, in the most frightful tortures that Satan could suggest to the imagination of a savage; Father Charles Garnier pierced with three bullets, and giving up the ghost while blessing his converts; Father de Noue dying on his knees in the snow!

These missions had succumbed in 1648 and 1649 under the attacks of the Iroquois. The venerable founder of St. Sulpice, M. Olier, had foreseen this misfortune; he had always doubted the success of missions so extended and so widely scattered without a centre of support sufficiently strong to resist a systematic and concerted attack of all their enemies at once. Without disapproving the despatch of these flying columns of missionaries which visited tribe after tribe (perhaps the only possible method in a country governed by pagan chiefs), he believed that another system of preaching the gospel would produce, perhaps with less danger, a more durable effect in the regions protected by the flag of France. Taking up again the thought of the Benedictine monks, who have succeeded so well in other countries, M. Olier and the other founders of Montreal wished to establish a centre of fervent piety which should accomplish still more by example than by preaching. The development and progress of religious work must increase with the material importance of this centre of proselytism. In consequence, success would be slow, less brilliant, but surer than that ordinarily obtained by separate missions. This was, at least, the hope of our fathers, and we of Quebec would seem unjust towards Providence and towards them if, beholding the present condition of the two seminaries of this city, of our Catholic colleges, of our institutions of every kind, and of our religious orders, we did not recognize that their thought was wise, and their enterprise one of prudence and blessed by God.

Up to 1658 New France belonged to the jurisdiction of the Bishops of St. Malo and of Rouen. At the time of the second voyage of

Cartier, in 1535, his whole crew, with their officers at their head, confessed and received communion from the hands of the Bishop of St. Malo. This jurisdiction lasted until the appointment of the first Bishop of New France. The creation of a diocese came in due time; the need of an ecclesiastical superior, of a character capable of imposing his authority made itself felt more and more. Disorders of all kinds crept into the colony, and our fathers felt the necessity of a firm and vigorous arm to remedy this alarming state of affairs. The love of lucre, of gain easily acquired by the sale of spirituous liquors to the savages, brought with it evils against which the missionaries endeavoured to react.

François de Laval-Montmorency, who was called in his youth the Abbé de Montigny, was, on the recommendation of the Jesuits, appointed apostolic vicar by Pope Alexander VII, who conferred upon him the title of Bishop of Petræa in partibus. The Church in Canada was then directly connected with the Holy See, and the sovereign pontiff abandoned to the king of France the right of appointment and presentation of bishops having the authority of apostolic vicars.

The difficulties which arose between Mgr. de Laval and the Abbé de Queylus, Grand Vicar of Rouen for Canada, were regrettable, but, thanks to the truly apostolic zeal and the purity of intention of these two men of God, these difficulties were not long in giving place to a noble rivalry for good, fostered by a perfect harmony. The Abbé de Queylus had come to take possession of the Island of Montreal for the company of St. Sulpice, and to establish there a seminary on the model of that in Paris. This creation, with that of the hospital established by Mlle. Mance, gave a great impetus to the young city of Montreal. Moreover, religion was so truly the motive of the foundation of the colony by M. Olier and his associates, that the latter had placed the Island of Montreal under the protection of the Holy Virgin. The priests of St. Sulpice, who had become the lords of the island, had already given an earnest of their labours; they too aspired to venerate martyrs chosen from their ranks, and in the same year MM. Lemaître and Vignal perished at the hands of the wild Iroquois.

Meanwhile, under the paternal direction of Mgr. de Laval, and the thoroughly Christian administration of governors like Champlain, de Montmagny, d'Ailleboust, or of leaders like Maisonneuve and Major Closse, Heaven was pleased to spread its blessings upon the rising colony; a number of savages asked and received baptism, and the fervour of the colonists endured. The men were not the only ones to spread the good word; holy maidens worked on their part for the glory of God, whether in the hospitals of Quebec and Montreal, or in the institution of the Ursulines in the heart of the city of Champlain, or, finally, in the modest school founded at Ville-Marie by Sister Marguerite Bourgeoys. It is true that the blood of the Indians and of their missionaries had been shed in floods, that the Huron missions had been exterminated, and that, moreover, two camps of Algonquins had been destroyed and swept away; but nations as well as individuals may promise themselves the greater progress in the spiritual life according as they commence it with a more abundant and a richer record; and the greatest treasure of a nation is the blood of the martyrs who have founded it. Moreover, the fugitive Hurons went to convert their enemies, and even from the funeral pyres of the priests was to spring the spark of faith for all these peoples. Two hamlets were founded for the converted Iroquois, those of the Sault St. Louis (Caughnawaga) and of La Montagne at Montreal, and fervent neophytes gathered there.

Certain historians have regretted that the first savages encountered by the French in North America should have been Hurons; an alliance made with the Iroquois, they say, would have been a hundred times more profitable for civilization and for France. What do we know about it? Man imagines and arranges his plans, but above these arrangements hovers Providence—fools say, chance—whose foreseeing hand sets all in order for the accomplishment of His impenetrable design. Yet, however firmly convinced the historian may be that the eye of Providence never sleeps, that the Divine Hand is never still, he must be sober in his observations; he must yield neither to his fancy nor to his imagination; but neither must he banish God from history, for then everything in it would become incomprehensible and inexplicable, absurd and barren. It was this same God who guides events at His will that inspired and sustained the devoted missionaries in their efforts against the revenue-farmers in the matter of the sale of intoxicating liquors to the savages. The struggle which they maintained, supported by the venerable Bishop of Petræa, is wholly to their honour; it was a question of saving even against their will the unfortunate children of the woods who were addicted to the fatal passion of intoxication. Unhappily, the Governors d'Avaugour and de Mézy, in supporting the greed of the traders, were perhaps right from the political point of view, but certainly wrong from a philanthropic and Christian standpoint.

The colony continuing to prosper, and the growing need of a national clergy becoming more and more felt, Mgr. de Laval founded in 1663 a seminary at Quebec. The king decided that the tithes raised from the colonists should be collected by the seminary, which was to provide for the maintenance of the priests and for divine service in the established parishes. The Sovereign Council fixed the tithe at a twenty-sixth.

The missionaries continued, none the less, to spread the light of the gospel and Christian civilization. It seems that the field of their labour had never been too vast for their desire. Ever onward! was their motto. While Fathers Garreau and Mesnard found death among the Algonquins on the coasts of Lake Superior, the Sulpicians Dollier and Gallinée were planting the cross on the shores of Lake Erie; Father Claude Allouez was preaching the gospel beyond Lake Superior; Fathers Dablon, Marquette, and Druillètes were establishing the mission of Sault Ste. Marie; Father Albanel was proceeding to explore Hudson Bay; Father Marquette, acting with Joliet, was following the course of the Mississippi as far as Arkansas; finally, later on, Father Arnaud accompanied La Vérendrye as far as the Rocky Mountains.

The establishment of the Catholic religion in Canada had now witnessed its darkest days; its history becomes intimately interwoven with that of the country. Up to the English conquest, the clergy and the different religious congregations, as faithful to France as to the Holy See, encouraged the Canadians in their struggles against the invaders. Accordingly, at the time of the invasion of the colony by Phipps, the Americans of Boston declared that they would spare neither monks nor missionaries if they succeeded in seizing Quebec; they bore a particular grudge against the priests of the seminary, to whom they ascribed the ravages committed shortly before in New England by theAbenaquis. They were punished for their boasting; forty seminarists assembled at St. Joachim, the country house of the seminary, joined the volunteers who fought at Beauport, and contributed so much to the victory that Frontenac, to recompense their bravery, presented them with a cannon captured by themselves.

The Church of Rome had been able to continue in peace its mission in Canada from the departure of Mgr. de Laval, in 1684, to the conquest of the country by the English. The worthy Bishop of Petræa, created Bishop of Quebec in 1674, was succeeded by Mgr. de St. Vallier, then by Mgr. de Mornay, who did not come to Canada, by Mgr. de Dosquet, Mgr. Pourroy de l'Aube-Rivière, and Mgr. de Pontbriant, who died the very year in which General de Lévis made of his flags on St. Helen's Island a sacred pyre.

In 1760 the Protestant religion was about to penetrate into Canada in the train of the victorious armies of Great Britain, having been proscribed in the colony from the time of Champlain. With conquerors of a different religion, the rôle of the Catholic clergy became much more arduous and delicate; this will be readily admitted when we recall that Mgr. Briand was informally apprised at the time of his appointment that the government of England would appear to be ignorant of his consecration and induction by the Bishop of Rome. But the clergy managed to keep itself on a level with its task. A systematic opposition on its part to the new masters of the country could only have drawn upon the whole population a bitter oppression, and we would not behold to-day the prosperity of these nine ecclesiastical provinces of Canada, with their twenty-four dioceses, these numerous parishes which vie with each other in the advancement of souls, these innumerable religious houses which everywhere are spreading education or charity. The Act of Quebec in 1774 delivered our fathers from the unjust fetters fastened on their freedom by the oath required under the Supremacy Act; but it is to the prudence of Mgr. Plessis in particular that Catholics owe the religious liberty which they now enjoy.

To-day, when passions are calmed, when we possess a full and complete liberty of conscience, to-day when the different religious denominations live side by side in mutual respect and tolerance of each other's convictions, let us give thanks to the spiritual guides who by their wisdom and moderation, but also by their energetic resistance when it was necessary, knew how to preserve for us our language and our religion. Let us always respect the worthy prelates who, like those who direct us to-day, edify us by their tact, their knowledge and their virtues.

CHAPTER II

THE EARLY YEARS OF FRANÇOIS DE LAVAL

Certain great men pass through the world like meteors; their brilliance, lightning-like at their first appearance, continues to cast a dazzling gleam across the centuries: such were Alexander the Great, Mozart, Shakespeare and Napoleon. Others, on the contrary, do not instantly command the admiration of the masses; it is necessary, in order that their transcendent merit should appear, either that the veil which covered their actions should be gradually lifted, or that, some fine day, and often after their death, the results of their work should shine forth suddenly to the eyes of men and prove their genius: such were Socrates, Themistocles, Jacquard, Copernicus, and Christopher Columbus.

The illustrious ecclesiastic who has given his name to our French-Canadian university, respected as he was by his contemporaries, has been esteemed at his proper value only by posterity. The reason is easy to understand: a colony still in its infancy is subject to many fluctuations before all the wheels of government move smoothly, and Mgr. de Laval, obliged to face ever renewed conflicts of authority, had necessarily either to abandon what he considered it his duty to support, or create malcontents. If sometimes he carried persistence to the verge of obstinacy, he must be judged in relation to the period in which he lived: governors like Frontenac were only too anxious to imitate their absolute master, whose guiding maxim was, "I am the state!" Moreover, where are the men of true worth who have not found upon their path the poisoned fruits of hatred? The so-called praise that is sometimes applied to a man, when we say of him, "he has not a single enemy," seems to us, on the contrary, a certificate of insignificance and obscurity. The figure of this great servant of God is one of those which shed the most glory on the history of Canada; the age of Louis XIV, so marvellous in the number of great men which it gave to France, lavished them also upon her daughter of the new continent—Brébeuf and Lalemant, de Maisonneuve, Dollard, Laval, Talon, de la Salle, Frontenac, d'Iberville, de Maricourt, de Sainte-Hélène, and many others.

"Noble as a Montmorency" says a well-known adage. The founder of that illustrious line, Bouchard, Lord of Montmorency, figures as early as 950 a.d. among the great vassals of the kingdom of France. The heads of this house bore formerly the titles of First Christian Barons and of First Barons of France; it became allied to several royal houses, and gave to the elder daughter of the Church several cardinals, six constables, twelve marshals, four admirals, and a great number of distinguished generals and statesmen. Sprung from this family, whose origin is lost in the night of time, François de Laval-Montmorency was born at Montigny-sur-Avre, in the department of Eure-et-Loir, on April 30th, 1623. This charming village, which still exists, was part of the important diocese of Chartres. Through his father, Hugues de Laval, Seigneur of Montigny, Montbeaudry, Alaincourt and Revercourt, the future Bishop of Quebec traced his descent from Count Guy de Laval, younger son of the constable Mathieu de Montmorency, and through his mother, Michelle de Péricard, he belonged to a family of hereditary officers of the Crown, which was well-known in Normandy, and gave to the Church a goodly number of prelates.

Like St. Louis, one of the protectors of his ancestors, the young François was indebted to his mother for lessons and examples of piety and of charity which he never forgot. Virtue, moreover, was as natural to the Lavals as bravery on the field of battle, and whether it were in the retinue of Clovis, when the First Barons received the regenerating water of baptism, or on the immortal plain of Bouvines; whether it were by the side of Blanche of Castile, attacked by the rebellious nobles, or in the terrible holocaust of Crécy; whether it were in the *fight of the giants* at Marignan, or after Pavia during the captivity of the *roi-gentilhomme*; everywhere where country and religion appealed to their defenders one was sure of hearing shouted in the foremost ranks the motto of the Montmorencys: *"Dieu ayde au premier baron chrétien!"*

Young Laval received at the baptismal font the name of the heroic missionary to the Indies, François-Xavier. To this saint and to the founder of the Franciscans, François d'Assise, he devoted throughout his life an ardent worship. Of his youth we hardly know anything except the misfortunes which happened to his family. He was only fourteen years old when, in 1636, he suffered the loss of his father, and one of his near kinsmen, Henri de Montmorency, grand marshal of France, and governor of Languedoc, beheaded by the order of Richelieu. The bravery displayed by this valiant warrior in battle unfortunately did not redeem the fault which he had committed in rebelling against the established power, against his lawful master, Louis XIII, and in neglecting thus the traditions handed down to him by his family through more than seven centuries of glory.

Some historians reproach Richelieu with cruelty, but in that troublous age when, hardly free from the wars of religion, men rushed carelessly on into the rebellions of the duc d'Orléans and the duc de Soissons, into the conspiracies of Chalais, of Cinq-Mars and de Thou, soon followed by the war of La Fronde, it was not by an indulgence synonymous with weakness that it was possible to strengthen the royal power. Who knows if it was not this energy of the great cardinal which inspired the young François, at an age when sentiment is so deeply impressed upon the soul, with those ideas of firmness which distinguished him later on?

The future Bishop of Quebec was then a scholar in the college of La Flèche, directed by the Jesuits, for his pious parents held nothing dearer than the education of their children in the fear of God and love of the good. They had had six children; the two first had perished in the flower of their youth on fields of battle; François, who was now the eldest, inherited the name and patrimony of Montigny, which he gave up later on to his brother Jean-Louis, which explains why he was called for some time Abbé de Montigny, and resumed later the generic name of the family of Laval; the fifth son, Henri de Laval, joined the Benedictine monks and became prior of La Croix-Saint-Leuffroy. Finally the only sister of Mgr. Laval, Anne Charlotte, became Mother Superior of the religious community of the Daughters of the Holy Sacrament.

François edified the comrades of his early youth by his ardent piety, and his tender respect for the house of God; his masters, too, clever as they were in the art of guiding young men and of distinguishing those who were to shine later on, were not slow in recognizing his splendid qualities, the clear-sightedness and breadth of his intelligence, and his wonderful memory. As a reward for his good conduct he was admitted to the privileged ranks of those who comprised the Congregation of the Holy Virgin. We know what good these admirable societies, founded by the sons of Loyola, have accomplished and still accomplish daily in Catholic schools the world over. Societies which vie with each other in piety and encouragement of virtue, they inspire young people with the love of prayer, the habits of regularity and of holy practices.

The congregation of the college of La Flèche had then the good fortune of being directed by Father Bagot, one of those superior priests always so numerous in the Company of Jesus. At one time confessor to King Louis XIII, Father Bagot was a profound philosopher and an eminent theologian. It was under his clever direction that the mind of François de Laval was formed, and we shall witness later the germination of the seed which the learned Jesuit sowed in the soul of his beloved scholar.

At this period great families devoted to God from early youth the younger members who showed inclination for the religious life. François was only nine years old when he received the tonsure, and fifteen when he was appointed canon of the cathedral of Evreux. Without the revenues which he drew from his prebend, he would not have been able to continue his literary studies; the death of his father, in fact, had left his family in a rather precarious condition of fortune. He was to remain to the end of his career the pupil of his preferred masters, for it was under them that, having at the age of nineteen left the institution where he had brilliantly completed his classical education, he studied philosophy and theology at the Collège de Clermont at Paris.

He was plunged in these noble studies, when two terrible blows fell upon him; he learned of the successive deaths of his two eldest brothers, who had fallen gloriously, one at Freiburg, the other at Nördlingen. He became thus the head of the family, and as if the temptations which this title offered him were not sufficient, bringing him as it did, together with a great name a brilliant future, his mother came, supported by the Bishop of Evreux, his cousin, to beg him to abandon the ecclesiastical career and to marry, in order to maintain the honour of his house. Many others would have succumbed, but what were temporal advantages to a man who had long aspired to the glory of going to preach the Divine Word in far-off missions? He remained inflexible; all that his mother could obtain from him was his consent to devote to her for some time his clear judgment and intellect in setting in order the affairs of his family. A few months sufficed for success in this task. In order to place an impassable abyss between himself and the world, he made a full and complete renunciation in favour of his brother Jean-Louis of his rights of primogeniture and all his titles to the seigniory of Montigny and Montbeaudry. The world is ever prone to admire a chivalrous action, and to look askance at deeds which appear to savour of fanaticism. To Laval this renunciation of worldly wealth and honour appeared in the simple light of duty. His Master's words were inspiration enough: "Wist ye not that I must be about my Father's business?"

Returning to the Collège de Clermont, he now thought of nothing but of preparing to receive worthily the holy orders. It was on September rd, 1647, at Paris, that he saw dawn for him the beautiful day of the first mass, whose memory perfumes the whole life of the priest. We may guess with what fervour he must have ascended the steps of the holy altar; if up to that moment he had merely loved his God, he must on that day have dedicated to Jesus all the powers of his being, all the tenderness of his soul, and his every heart-beat.

Mgr. de Péricard, Bishop of Evreux, was not present at the ordination of his cousin; death had taken him away, but before expiring, besides expressing his regret to the new priest for having tried at the time, thinking to further the aims of God, to dissuade him from the ecclesiastical life, he gave him a last proof of his affection by appointing him archdeacon of his cathedral. The duties of the archdeaconry of Evreux, comprising, as it did, nearly one hundred and sixty parishes, were particularly heavy, yet the young priest fulfilled them for seven years, and M. de la Colombière explains to us how he acquitted himself of them: "The regularity of his visits, the fervour of his enthusiasm, the improvement and the good order which he established in the parishes, the relief of the poor, his interest in all sorts of charity, none of which escaped his notice: all this showed well that without being a bishop he had the ability and merit of one, and that there was no service which the Church might not expect from so great a subject."

But our future Bishop of New France aspired to more glorious fields. One of those zealous apostles who were evangelizing India at this period, Father Alexander of Rhodes, asked from the sovereign pontiff the appointment for Asia of three French bishops, and submitted to the Holy See the names of MM. Pallu, Picquet and Laval. There was no question of hesitation. All three set out immediately for Rome. They remained there fifteen months; the opposition of the Portuguese court caused the failure of this plan, and François de Laval returned to France. He had resigned the office of archdeacon the year before, 1653, in favour of a man of tried virtue, who had been, nevertheless, a prey to calumny and persecution, the Abbé Henri-Marie Boudon; thus freed from all responsibility, Laval could satisfy his desire of preparing himself by prayer for the designs which God might have for him.

In his desire of attaining the greatest possible perfection, he betook himself to Caen, to the religious retreat of M. de Bernières. St. Vincent de Paul, who had trained M. Olier, was desirous also that his pupil, before going to find a field for his apostolic zeal among the people of Auvergne, should prepare himself by earnest meditation in retirement at St. Lazare. "Silence and introspection seemed to St. Vincent," says M. de Lanjuère, the author of the life of M. Olier, "the first conditions of success, preceding any serious enterprise. He had not learned this from Pythagoras or the Greek philosophers, who were, indeed, so careful to prescribe for their disciples a long period of meditation before initiation into their systems, nor even from the experience of all superior men, who, in order to ripen a great plan or to evolve a great thought, have always felt the need of isolation in the nobler acceptance of the word; but he had this maxim from the very example of the Saviour, who, before the temptation and before the transfiguration, withdrew from the world in order to contemplate, and who prayed in Gethsemane before His death on the cross, and who often led His disciples into solitude to rest, and to listen to His most precious communications."

In this little town of Caen, in a house called the Hermitage, lived Jean de Bernières of Louvigny, together with some of his friends. They had gathered together for the purpose of aiding each other in mutual sanctification; they practised prayer, and lived in the exercise of the highest piety and charity. François de Laval passed three years in this Hermitage, and his wisdom was already so highly appreciated, that during the period of his stay he was entrusted with two important missions, whose successful issue attracted attention to him and led naturally to his appointment to the bishopric of Canada.

As early as 1647 the king foresaw the coming creation of a bishopric in New France, for he constituted the Upper Council "of the Governor of Quebec, the Governor of Montreal and the Superior of the Jesuits, *until there should be a bishop.*" A few years later, in 1656, the Company of Montreal obtained from M. Olier, the pious founder of the Seminary of St. Sulpice, the services of four of his priests for the colony, under the direction of one of them, M. de Queylus, Abbé de Loc-Dieu, whose brilliant qualities, as well as the noble use which he made of his great fortune, marked him out naturally as the probable choice of his associates for the episcopacy. But the Jesuits, in possession of all the missions of New France, had their word to say, especially since the mitre had been offered by the queen regent, Anne of Austria, to one of their number, Father Léjeune, who had not, however, been able to accept, their rules forbidding it. They had then proposed to the court of France and the court of Rome the name of François de Laval; but believing that the colony was not ready for the erection of a see, they expressed the opinion that the sending of an apostolic vicar with the functions and powers of a bishop *in partibus* would suffice. Moreover, if the person sent should not succeed, he could at any time be recalled, which could not be done in the case of a bishop. Alexander VII had given his consent to this new plan, and Mgr. de Laval was consecrated by the nuncio of the Pope at Paris, on Sunday, December 8th, 1658, in the church of St. Germain-des-Prés. After having taken, with the assent of the sovereign pontiff, the oath of fidelity to the king, the new Bishop of Petræa said farewell to his pious mother (who died in that same year) and embarked at La Rochelle in the month of April, 1659. The only property he retained was an income of a thousand francs assured to him by the Queen-Mother; but he was setting out to conquer treasures very different from those coveted by the Spanish adventurers who sailed to Mexico and Peru. He arrived on June 16th at Quebec, with letters from the king which enjoined upon all the recognition of Mgr. de Laval of Petræa as being authorized to exercise episcopal functions in the colony without prejudice to the rights of the Archbishop of Rouen.

Unfortunately, men's minds were not very certain then as to the title and qualities of an apostolic vicar. They asked themselves if he were not a simple delegate whose authority did not conflict with the jurisdiction of the two grand vicars of the Jesuits and the

Sulpicians. The communities, at first divided on this point, submitted on the receipt of new letters from the king, which commanded the recognition of the sole authority of the Bishop of Petræa. The two grand vicars obeyed, and M. de Queylus came to Quebec, where he preached the sermon on St. Augustine's Day (August 28th), and satisfied the claim to authority of the apostolic vicar.

But a new complication arose: the *St. André*, which had arrived on September 7th, brought to the Abbé de Queylus a new appointment as grand vicar from the Archbishop of Rouen, which contained his protests at court against the apostolic vicar, and letters from the king which seemed to confirm them. Doubt as to the authenticity of the powers of Mgr. de Laval might thus, at least, seem permissible; no act of the Abbé de Queylus, however, indicates that it was openly manifested, and the very next month the abbé returned to France.

We may understand, however, that Mgr. de Laval, in the midst of such difficulties, felt the need of early asserting his authority. He promulgated an order enjoining upon all the secular ecclesiastics of the country the disavowal of all foreign jurisdictions and the recognition of his alone, and commanded them to sign this regulation in evidence of their submission. All signed it, including the devoted priests of St. Sulpice at Montreal.

Two years later, nevertheless, the Abbé de Queylus returned with bulls from the Congregation of the Daterie at Rome. These bulls placed him in possession of the parish of Montreal. In spite of the formal forbiddance of the Bishop of Petræa, he undertook, strong in what he judged to be his rights, to betake himself to Montreal. The prelate on his side believed that it was his duty to take severe steps, and he suspended the Abbé de Queylus. On instructions which were given him by the king, Governor d'Avaugour transmitted to the Abbé de Queylus an order to return to France. The court of Rome finally settled the question by giving the entire jurisdiction of Canada to Mgr. de Laval. The affair thus ended, the Abbé de Queylus returned to the colony in 1668. The population of Ville-Marie received with deep joy this benefactor, to whose generosity it owed so much, and on his side the worthy Bishop of Petræa proved that if he had believed it his duty to defend his own authority when menaced, he had too noble a heart to preserve a petty rancour. He appointed the worthy Abbé de Queylus his grand vicar at Montreal.

When for the first time Mgr. de Laval set foot on the soil of America, the people, assembled to pay respect to their first pastor, were struck by his address, which was both affable and majestic, by his manners, as easy as they were distinguished, but especially by that charm which emanates from every one whose heart has remained ever pure. A lofty brow indicated an intellect above the ordinary; the clean-cut long nose was the inheritance of the Montmorencys; his eye was keen and bright; his eyebrows strongly arched; his thin lips and prominent chin showed a tenacious will; his hair was scanty; finally, according to the custom of that period, a moustache and chin beard added to the strength and energy of his features. From the moment of his arrival the prelate produced the best impression. "I cannot," said Governor d'Argenson, "I cannot highly enough esteem the zeal and piety of Mgr. of Petræa. He is a true man of prayer, and I make no doubt that his labours will bear goodly fruits in this country." Boucher, governor of Three Rivers, wrote thus: "We have a bishop whose zeal and virtue are beyond anything that I can say."

CHAPTER III

THE SOVEREIGN COUNCIL

The pious bishop who is the subject of this study was not long in proving that his virtues were not too highly esteemed. An ancient vessel, the *St. André*, brought from France two hundred and six persons, among whom were Mlle. Mance, the foundress of the Montreal hospital, Sister Bourgeoys, and two Sulpicians, MM. Vignal and Lemaître. Now this ship had long served as a sailors' hospital, and it had been sent back to sea without the necessary quarantine. Hardly had its passengers lost sight of the coasts of France when the plague broke out among them, and with such intensity that all were more or less attacked by it; Mlle. Mance, in particular, was almost immediately reduced to the point of death. Always very delicate, and exhausted by a preceding voyage, she did not seem destined to resist this latest attack. Moreover, all aid was lacking, even the rations of fresh water ran short, and from a fear of contagion, which will be readily understood, but which was none the less disastrous, the captain at first forbade the Sisters of Charity who were on board to minister to the sick. This precaution cost seven or eight of these unfortunate people their lives. At least M. Vignal and M. Lemaître, though both suffering themselves, were able to offer to the dying the consolations of their holy office. M. Lemaître, more vigorous than his colleague, and possessed of an admirable energy and devotion, was not satisfied merely with encouraging and ministering to the unfortunate in their last moments, but even watched over their remains at the risk of his own life; he buried them piously, wound them in their shrouds, and said over them the final prayers as they were lowered into the sea. Two Huguenots, touched by his devotion, died in the Roman Catholic faith. The Sisters were finally permitted to exercise their charitable office. Although ill, they as well as Sister Bourgeoys, displayed a heroic energy, and raised the morale of all the unfortunate passengers.

To this sickness were added other sufferings incident to such a voyage, and frightful storms did not cease to attack the ship until its entry into the Gulf of St. Lawrence. Several times they believed themselves on the point of foundering, and the two priests gave absolution to all. The tempest carried these unhappy people so far from their route that they did not arrive at Quebec until September 7th, exhausted by disease, famine and trials of all sorts. Father Dequen, of the Society of Jesus, showed in this matter an example of the most admirable charity. He brought to the sick refreshments and every manner of aid, and lavished upon all the offices of his holy ministry. As a result of his self-devotion, he was attacked by the scourge and died in the exercise of charity. Several more, after being conveyed to the hospital, succumbed to the disease, and the whole country was infected. Mgr. of Petræa was admirable in his devotion; he hardly left the hospital at all, and constituted himself the nurse of all these unfortunates, making their beds and giving them the most attentive care. "He is continually at the hospital," wrote Mother Mary of the Incarnation, "in order to help the sick and to make their beds. We do what we can to prevent him and to shield his health, but no eloquence can dissuade him from these acts of self-abasement."

In the spring of the year 1662, Mgr. de Laval rented for his own use an old house situated on the site of the present parochial residence at Quebec, and it was there that, with the three other priests who then composed his episcopal court, he edified all the colonists by the simplicity of a cenobitic life. He had been at first the guest of the Jesuit Fathers, was later sheltered by the Sisters of the Hôtel-Dieu, and subsequently lodged with the Ursulines. At this period it was indeed incumbent upon him to adapt himself to circumstances; nor did these modest conditions displease the former pupil of M. de Bernières, since, as Latour bears witness, "he always complained that people did too much for him; he showed a distaste for all that was too daintily prepared, and affected, on the contrary, a sort of avidity for coarser fare." Mother Mary of the Incarnation wrote: "He lives like a holy man and an apostle; his life is so exemplary that he commands the admiration of the country. He gives everything away and lives like a pauper, and one may well say that he has the very spirit of poverty. He practises this poverty in his house, in his manner of living, and in the matter of furniture and servants; for he has but one gardener, whom he lends to poor people when they have need of him, and a valet who formerly served M. de Bernières."

But if the reverend prelate was modest and simple in his personal tastes, he became inflexible when he thought it his duty to maintain the rights of the Church. And he watched over these rights with the more circumspection since he was the first bishop installed in the colony, and was unwilling to allow abuses to be planted there, which later it would be very difficult, not to say impossible, to uproot. Hence the continual friction between him and the governor-general, d'Argenson, on questions of precedence and etiquette. Some of these disputes would seem to us childish to-day if even such a writer as Parkman did not put us on our guard against a premature judgment.[1] "The disputes in question," writes Parkman, "though of a nature to provoke a smile on irreverent lips, were by no means so puerile as they appear. It is difficult in a modern democratic society to conceive the substantial importance of the signs and symbols of dignity and authority, at a time and among a people where they were adjusted with the most scrupulous precision, and accepted by all classes as exponents of relative degrees in the social and political scale. Whether the bishop or the governor should sit in the higher seat at table thus became a political question, for it defined to the popular understanding the position of Church and State in their relations to government."

In his zeal for making his episcopal authority respected, could not the prelate, however, have made some concessions to the temporal power? It is allowable to think so, when his panegyrist, the Abbé Gosselin, acknowledges it in these terms: "Did he sometimes show too much ardour in the settlement of a question or in the assertion of his rights? It is possible. As the Abbé Ferland rightly observes, 'no virtue is perfect upon earth.' But he was too pious and too disinterested for us to suspect for a moment the purity of his intentions." In certain passages in his journal Father Lalemant seems to be of the same opinion. All men are fallible; even the greatest saints have erred. In this connection the remark of St. Bernardin of Siena presents itself naturally to the religious mind: "Each time," says he, "that God grants to a creature a marked and particular favour, and when divine grace summons him to a special task and to some sublime position, it is a rule of Providence to furnish that creature with all the means necessary to fulfil the mission which is entrusted to him, and to bring it to a happy conclusion. Providence prepares his birth, directs his education, produces the environment in which he is to live; even his faults Providence will use in the accomplishment of its purposes."

Difficulties of another sort fixed between the spiritual and the temporal chiefs of the colony a still deeper gulf; they arose from the trade in brandy with the savages. It had been formerly forbidden by the Sovereign Council, and this measure, urged by the clergy and the missionaries, put a stop to crimes and disorders. However, for the purpose of gain, certain men infringed this wise prohibition, and Mgr. de Laval, aware of the extensive harm caused by the fatal passion of the Indians for intoxicating liquors, hurled excommunication against all who should carry on the traffic in brandy with the savages. "It would be very difficult," writes M. de Latour, "to realize to what an excess these barbarians are carried by drunkenness. There is no species of madness, of crime or inhumanity to which they do not descend. The savage, for a glass of brandy, will give even his clothes, his cabin, his wife, his children; a squaw when made drunk—and this is often done purposely—will abandon herself to the first comer. They will tear each other to pieces. If one enters a cabin whose inmates have just drunk brandy, one will behold with astonishment and horror the father cutting the throat of his son, the son threatening his father; the husband and wife, the best of friends, inflicting murderous blows upon each other, biting each other, tearing out each other's eyes, noses and ears; they are no longer recognizable, they are madmen; there is perhaps in the world no more vivid picture of hell. There are often some among them who seek drunkenness in order to avenge themselves upon their enemies, and commit with impunity all sorts of crimes under the pretext of this fine excuse, which passes with them for a complete justification, that at these times they are not free and not in their senses." Drunken savages are brutes, it is true, but were not the whites who fostered this fatal passion of intoxication more guilty still than the wretches whom they ignominiously urged on to vice? Let us see what the same writer says of these corrupters. "If it is difficult," says he, "to explain the excesses of the savage, it is also difficult to understand the extent of the greed, the hypocrisy and the rascality of those who supply them with these drinks. The facility for making immense profits which is afforded them by the ignorance and the passions of these people, and the certainty of impunity, are things which they cannot resist; the attraction of gain acts upon them as drunkenness does upon their victims. How many crimes arise from the same source? There is no mother who does not fear for her daughter, no husband who does not dread for his wife, a libertine armed with a bottle of brandy; they rob and pillage these wretches, who, stupefied by intoxication when they are not maddened by it, can neither refuse nor defend themselves. There is no barrier which is not forced, no weakness which is not exploited, in these remote regions where, without either witnesses or masters, only the voice of brutal passion is listened to, every crime of which is inspired by a glass of brandy. The French are worse in this respect than the savages."

Governor d'Avaugour supported energetically the measures taken by Mgr. de Laval; unfortunately a regrettable incident destroyed the harmony between their two authorities. Inspired by his good heart, the superior of the Jesuits, Father Lalemant, interceded with the governor in favour of a woman imprisoned for having infringed the prohibition of the sale of brandy to the Indians. "If she is not to be punished," brusquely replied d'Avaugour, "no one shall be punished henceforth!" And, as he made it a point of honour not to withdraw this unfortunate utterance, the traders profited by it. From that time license was no longer bridled; the savages got drunk, the traders were enriched, and the colony was in jeopardy. Sure of being supported by the governor, the merchants listened to neither bishop nor missionaries. Grieved at seeing his prayers as powerless as his commands, Mgr. de Laval decided to carry his complaint to the foot of the throne, and he set sail for France in the autumn of 1662. "Statesmen who place the freedom of commerce above morality of action," says Jacques de Beaudoncourt, "still consider that the bishop was wrong, and see in this matter a fine opportunity to inveigh against the encroachments of the clergy; but whoever has at heart the cause of human dignity will not hesitate to take the side of the missionaries who sought to preserve the savages from the vices which have brought about their ruin and their disappearance. The Montagnais race, which is still the most important in Canada, has been preserved by Catholicism from the vices and the misery which brought about so rapidly the extirpation of the savages."

Mgr. de Laval succeeded beyond his hopes; cordially received by King Louis XIV, he obtained the recall of Governor d'Avaugour.

But this purpose was not the only one which he had made the goal of his ambition; he had in view another, much more important for the welfare of the colony. Fourteen years before, the Iroquois had exterminated the Hurons, and since this period the colonists had not enjoyed a single hour of calm; the devotion of Dollard and of his sixteen heroic comrades had narrowly saved them from a horrible danger. The worthy prelate obtained from the king a sufficiently large assignment of troops to deliver the colony at last from its most dangerous enemies. "We expect next year," he wrote to the sovereign pontiff, "twelve hundred soldiers, with whom, by God's help, we shall try to overcome the fierce Iroquois. The Marquis de Tracy will come to Canada in order to see for himself the measures which are necessary to make of New France a strong and prosperous colony."

M. Dubois d'Avaugour was recalled, and yet he rendered before his departure a distinguished service to the colony. "The St. Lawrence," he wrote in a memorial to the monarch, "is the key to a country which may become the greatest state in the world. There should be sent to this colony three thousand soldiers, to be discharged after three years of service; they could make Quebec an impregnable fortress, subdue the Iroquois, build redoubtable forts on the banks of the Hudson, where the Dutch have only a wretched wooden hut, and in short, open for New France a road to the sea by this river." It was mainly this report which induced the sovereign to take back Canada from the hands of the Company of the Cent-Associés, who were incapable of colonizing it, and to reintegrate it in the royal domain.

Must we think with M. de la Colombière,[2] with M. de Latour and with Cardinal Taschereau, that the Sovereign Council was the work of Mgr. de Laval? We have some justification in believing it when we remember that the king arrived at this important decision while the energetic Laval was present at his court. However it may be, on April 24th, 1663, the Company of New France abandoned the colony to the royal government, which immediately created in Canada three courts of justice and above them the Sovereign Council as a court of appeal.

The Bishop of Petræa sailed in 1663 for North America with the new governor, M. de Mézy, who owed to him his appointment. His other fellow-passengers were M. Gaudais-Dupont, who came to take possession of the country in the name of the king, two priests, MM. Maizerets and Hugues Pommier, Father Rafeix, of the Society of Jesus, and three ecclesiastics. The passage was stormy and lasted four months. To-day, when we leave Havre and disembark a week later at New York, after having enjoyed all the refinements of luxury and comfort invented by an advanced but materialistic civilization, we can with difficulty imagine the discomforts, hardships and privations of four long months on a stormy sea. Scurvy, that fatal consequence of famine and exhaustion, soon broke out among the passengers, and many died of it. The bishop, himself stricken by the disease, did not cease, nevertheless, to lavish his care upon the unfortunates who were attacked by the infection; he even attended them at the hospital after they had landed.

The country was still at this time under the stress of the emotion caused by the terrible earthquake of 1663. Father Lalemant has left us a striking description of this cataclysm, marked by the naïve exaggeration of the period: "It was February 5th, 1663, about half-past five in the evening, when a great roar was heard at the same time throughout the extent of Canada. This noise, which gave the impression that fire had broken out in all the houses, made every one rush out of doors in order to flee from such a sudden conflagration. But instead of seeing smoke and flame, the people were much surprised to behold walls tottering, and all the stones moving as if they had become detached; the roofs seemed to bend downward on one side, then to lean over on the other; the bells rang of their own accord; joists, rafters and boards cracked, the earth quivered and made the stakes of the palisades dance in a manner which would appear incredible if we had not seen it in various places.

"Then every one rushes outside, animals take to flight, children cry through the streets, men and women, seized with terror, know not where to take refuge, thinking at every moment that they must be either overwhelmed in the ruins of the houses or buried in some abyss about to open under their feet; some, falling to their knees in the snow, cry for mercy; others pass the rest of the night in prayer, because the earthquake still continues with a certain undulation, almost like that of ships at sea, and such that some feel from these shocks the same sickness that they endure upon the water.

"The disorder was much greater in the forest. It seemed that there was a battle between the trees, which were hurled together, and not only their branches but even their trunks seemed to leave their places to leap upon each other with a noise and a confusion which made our savages say that the whole forest was drunk.

"There seemed to be the same combat between the mountains, of which some were uprooted and hurled upon the others, leaving great chasms in the places whence they came, and now burying the trees, with which they were covered, deep in the earth up to their tops, now thrusting them in, with branches downward, taking the place of the roots, so that they left only a forest of upturned trunks.

"While this general destruction was going on on land, sheets of ice five or six feet thick were broken and shattered to pieces, and split in many places, whence arose thick vapour or streams of mud and sand which ascended high into the air; our springs either flowed no longer or ran with sulphurous waters; the rivers were either lost from sight or became polluted, the waters of some becoming yellow, those of others red, and the great St. Lawrence appeared quite livid up to the vicinity of Tadousac, a most astonishing prodigy, and one capable of surprising those who know the extent of this great river below the Island of Orleans, and what matter must be necessary to whiten it.

"We behold new lakes where there never were any; certain mountains engulfed are no longer seen; several rapids have been smoothed out; not a few rivers no longer appear; the earth is cleft in many places, and has opened abysses which seem to have no bottom. In short, there has been produced such a confusion of woods upturned and buried, that we see now stretches of country of more than a thousand acres wholly denuded, and as if they were freshly ploughed, where a little before there had been but forests.

"Moreover, three circumstances made this earthquake most remarkable. The first is the time of its duration, since it lasted into the month of August, that is to say, more than six months. It is true that the shocks were not always so rude; in certain places, for example, towards the mountains at the back of us, the noise and the commotion were long continued; at others, as in the direction of Tadousac, there was a quaking as a rule two or three times a day, accompanied by a great straining, and we noticed that in the higher places the disturbance was less than in the flat districts.

"The second circumstance concerns the extent of this earthquake, which we believe to have been universal throughout New France; for we learn that it was felt from Ile Percé and Gaspé, which are at the mouth of our river, to beyond Montreal, as likewise in New England, in Acadia and other very remote places; so that, knowing that the earthquake occurred throughout an extent of two hundred leagues in length by one hundred in breadth, we have twenty thousand square leagues of land which felt the earthquake on the same day and at the same moment.

"The third circumstance concerns God's particular protection of our homes, for we see near us great abysses and a prodigious extent of country wholly ruined, without our having lost a child or even a hair of our heads. We see ourselves surrounded by confusion and ruins, and yet we have had only a few chimneys demolished, while the mountains around us have been overturned."

From the point of view of conversions and returns to God the results were marvellous. "One can scarcely believe," says Mother Mary of the Incarnation, "the great number of conversions that God has brought about, both among infidels who have embraced the faith, and on the part of Christians who have abandoned their evil life. At the same time as God has shaken the mountains and the marble rocks of these regions, it would seem that He has taken pleasure in shaking consciences. Days of carnival have been changed into days of penitence and sadness; public prayers, processions and pilgrimages have been continual; fasts on bread and water very frequent; the general confessions more sincere than they would have been in the extremity of sickness. A single ecclesiastic, who directs the parish of Château-Richer, has assured us that he has procured more than eight hundred general confessions, and I leave you to think what the reverend Fathers must have accomplished who were day and night in the confessional. I do not think that in the whole country there is a single inhabitant who has not made a general confession. There have been inveterate sinners, who, to set their consciences at rest, have repeated their confession more than three times. We have seen admirable reconciliations, enemies falling on their knees before each other to ask each other's forgiveness, in so much sorrow that it was easy to see that these changes were the results of grace and of the mercy of God rather than of His justice."

[1] *The Old Régime in Canada*, p. 110.

[2]Joseph Séré de la Colombière, vicar-general and archdeacon of Quebec, pronounced Mgr. de Laval's funeral oration.

CHAPTER IV

ESTABLISHMENT OF THE SEMINARY

No sooner had he returned, than the Bishop of Petræa devoted all the strength of his intellect to the execution of a plan which he had long meditated, namely, the foundation of a seminary. In order to explain what he understood by this word we cannot do better than to quote his own ordinance relating to this matter: "There shall be educated and trained such young clerics as may appear fit for the service of God, and they shall be taught for this purpose the proper manner of administering the sacraments, the methods of apostolic catechism and preaching, moral theology, the ceremonies of the Church, the Gregorian chant, and other things belonging to the duties of a good ecclesiastic; and besides, in order that there may be formed in the said seminary and among its clergy a chapter composed of ecclesiastics belonging thereto and chosen from among us and the bishops of the said country, our successors, when the king shall have seen fit to found the seminary, or from those whom the said seminary may be able of itself to furnish to this institution through the blessing of God. We desire it to be a perpetual school of virtue, and a place of training whence we may derive pious and capable recruits, in order to send them on all occasions, and whenever there may be need, into the parishes and other places in the said country, in order to exercise therein priestly and other duties to which they may have been destined, and to withdraw them from the same parishes and duties when it may be judged fitting, reserving to ourselves always, and to the bishops, our successors in the said country, as well as to the said seminary, by our orders and those of the said lords bishops, the power of recalling all the ecclesiastics who may have gone forth as delegates into the parishes and other places, whenever it may be deemed necessary, without their having title or right of particular attachment to a parish, it being our desire, on the contrary, that they should be rightfully removable, and subject to dismissal and displacement at the will of the bishops and of the said seminary, by the orders of the same, in accordance with the sacred practice of the early ages of the Church, which is followed and preserved still at the present day in many dioceses of this kingdom."

Although this foregoing period is somewhat lengthy and a little obscure, so weighty with meaning is it, we have been anxious to quote it, first, because it is an official document, and because it came from the very pen of him whose life we are studying; and, secondly, because it shows that at this period serious reading, such as Cicero, Quintilian, and the Fathers of the Church, formed the mental pabulum of the people. In our days the beauty of a sentence is less sought after than its clearness and conciseness.

It may be well to add here the Abbé Gosselin's explanation of this *mandement*: "Three principal works are due to this document as the glorious inheritance of the seminary of Quebec. In the first place we have the natural work of any seminary, the training of ecclesiastics and the preparation of the clergy for priestly virtues. In the next place we have the creation of the chapter, which the Bishop of Petræa always considered important in a well organized diocese; it was his desire to find the elements of this chapter in his seminary, when the king should have provided for its endowment, or when the seminary itself could bear the expense.

Finally, there is that which in the mind of Mgr. de Laval was the supreme work of the seminary, its vital task: the seminary was to be not only a perpetual school of virtue, but also a place of supply on which he might draw for the persons needed in the administration of his diocese, and to which he might send them back when he should think best. All livings are connected with the seminary, but they are all transferable. The prelate here puts clearly and categorically the question of the transfer of livings. In his measures there is neither hesitation nor circumlocution. He does not seek to deceive the sovereign to whom he is about to submit his regulation. For him, in the present condition of New France, there can be no question of fixed livings; the priests must be by right removable, and subject to recall at the will of the bishop; and, as is fitting in a prelate worthy of the primitive Church, he always lays stress in his commands on the *holy practice of the early centuries*. The question was clearly put. It was as clearly understood by the sovereign, who approved some days later of the regulation of Mgr. de Laval."

It was in the month of April, 1663, that the worthy prelate had obtained the royal approval of the establishment of his seminary; it was on October 10th of the same year that he had it registered by the Sovereign Council.

A great difficulty arose: the missionaries, besides the help that they had obtained from the Company of the Cent-Associés, derived their resources from Europe; but how was the new secular clergy to be supported, totally lacking as it was in endowment and revenue? Mgr. de Laval resolved to employ the means adopted long ago by Charlemagne to assure the maintenance of the Frankish clergy: that of tithes or dues paid by the husbandman from his harvest. Accordingly he obtained from the king an ordinance according to which tithes, fixed at the amount of the thirteenth part of the harvests, should be collected from the colonists by the seminary; the latter was to use them for the maintenance of the priests, and for divine service in the established parishes. The burden was, perhaps, somewhat heavy. Mgr. de Laval, who, inspired by the spirit of poverty, had renounced his patrimony and lived solely upon a pension of a thousand francs which the queen paid him from her private exchequer, felt that he had a certain right to impose his disinterestedness upon others, but the colonists, sure of the support of the governor, M. de Mézy, complained.

The good understanding between the governor-general and the bishop had been maintained up to the end of January, 1664. Full of respect for the character and the virtue of his friend, M. de Mézy had energetically supported the ordinances of the Sovereign Council against the brandy traffic; he had likewise favoured the registration of the law of tithes, but the opposition which he met in the matter of an increase in his salary impelled him to arbitrary action. Of his own authority he displaced three councillors, and out of petty rancour allowed strong liquors to be sold to the savages. The open struggle between the bishop and himself produced the most unfavourable impression in the colony. The king decided that the matter must be brought to a head. M. de Courcelles was appointed governor, and, jointly with a viceroy, the Marquis de Tracy, and with the Intendant Talon, was entrusted with the investigation of the administration of M. de Mézy. They arrived a few months after the death of de Mézy, whom this untimely end saved perhaps from a well-deserved condemnation. He had become reconciled in his dying hour to his old and venerable friend, and the judges confined themselves to the erasure of the documents which recalled his administration.

The worthy Bishop of Petræa had not lost for a moment the confidence of the sovereign, as is proved by many letters which he received from the king and his prime minister, Colbert. "I send you by command of His Majesty," writes Colbert, "the sum of six thousand francs, to be disposed of as you may deem best to supply your needs and those of your Church. We cannot ascribe too great a value to a virtue like yours, which is ever equally maintained, which charitably extends its help wherever it is necessary, which makes you indefatigable in the functions of your episcopacy, notwithstanding the feebleness of your health and the frequent indispositions by which you are attacked, and which thus makes you share with the least of your ecclesiastics the task of administering the sacraments in places most remote from the principal settlements. I shall add nothing to this statement, which is entirely sincere, for fear of wounding your natural modesty, etc...." The prince himself is no less flattering: "My Lord Bishop of Petræa," writes Louis the Great, "I expected no less of your zeal for the exaltation of the faith, and of your affection for the furtherance of my service than the conduct observed by you in your important and holy mission. Its main reward is reserved by Heaven, which alone can recompense you in proportion to your merit, but you may rest assured that such rewards as depend on me will not be wanting at the fitting time. I subscribe, moreover, to my Lord Colbert's communications to you in my name."

Peace and harmony were re-established, and with them the hope of seeing finally disappear the constant menace of Iroquois forays. The magnificent regiment of Carignan, composed of six hundred men, reassured the colonists while it daunted their savage enemies. Thus three of the Five Nations hastened to sue for peace, and they obtained it. In order to protect the frontiers of the colony, M. de Tracy caused three forts to be erected on the Richelieu River, one at Sorel, another at Chambly, a third still more remote, that of Ste. Thérèse; then at the head of six hundred soldiers, six hundred militia and a hundred Indians, he marched towards the hamlets of the Mohawks. The result of this expedition was, unhappily, as fruitless as that of the later campaigns undertaken against the Indians by MM. de Denonville and de Frontenac. After a difficult march they come into touch with the savages; but these all flee into the woods, and they find only their huts stocked with immense supplies of corn for the winter, and a great number of pigs. At least, if they cannot reach the barbarians themselves, they can inflict upon them a terrible punishment; they set fire to the cabins and the corn, the pigs are slaughtered, and thus a large number of their wild enemies die of hunger during the winter. The viceroy was wise enough to accept the surrender of many Indians, and the peace which he concluded afforded the colony eighteen years of tranquillity.

The question of the apportionment of the tithes was settled in the following year, 1667. The viceroy, acting with MM. de Courcelles and Talon, decided that the tithe should be reduced to a twenty-sixth, by reason of the poverty of the inhabitants, and that newly-cleared lands should pay nothing for the first five years. Mgr. de Laval, ever ready to accept just and sensible measures, agreed to this decision. The revenues thus obtained were, none the less, insufficient, since the king subsequently gave eight or nine thousand francs to complete the endowment of the priests, whose annual salary was fixed at five hundred and seventy-four francs. In 1707 the sum granted by the French court was reduced to four thousand francs. If we remember that the French farmers contributed the thirteenth part of their harvest, that is to say, double the quantity of the Canadian tithe, for the support of their pastors, shall we deem excessive this modest tax raised from the colonists for men who devoted to them their time, their health, even their hours of rest, in order to procure for their parishioners the aid of religion? Is it not regrettable that too many among the colonists, who were yet such good Christians in the observance of religious practices, should have opposed an obstinate resistance to so righteous a demand? Can it be that, by a special dispensation of Heaven, the priests and vicars of Canada are not liable to the same material needs as ordinary mortals, and are they not obliged to pay in good current coin for their food, their medicines and their clothes?

The first seminary, built of stone,[3] rose in 1661 on the site of the present vicarage of the cathedral of Quebec; it cost eight thousand five hundred francs, two thousand of which were given by Mgr. de Laval. The first priest of Quebec and first superior of the seminary, M. Henri de Bernières, was able to occupy it in the autumn of the following year, and the Bishop of Petræa abode there from the time of his return from France on September 15th, 1663, until the burning of this house on November 15th, 1701. The first directors of the seminary were, besides M. de Bernières, MM. de Lauson-Charny, son of the former governor-general, Jean Dudouyt, Thomas Morel, Ange de Maizerets and Hugues Pommier. Except the first, who was a Burgundian, they were all born in the two provinces of Brittany and Normandy, the cradles of the majority of our ancestors.

The founder of the seminary had wished the livings to be transferable; later the government decided to the contrary, and the edict of 1679 decreed that the tithes should be payable only to the permanent priests; nevertheless the majority of them remained of their own free will attached to the seminary. They had learned there to practise a complete abnegation, and to give to the faithful the example of a united and fervent clerical family. "Our goods were held in common with those of the bishop," wrote M. de Maizerets, "I have never seen any distinction made among us between poor and rich, or the birth and rank of any one questioned, since we all consider each other as brothers."

The pious bishop himself set an example of disinterestedness; all that he had, namely an income of two thousand five hundred francs, which the Jesuits paid him as the tithes of the grain harvested upon their property, and a revenue of a thousand francs which he had from his friends in France, went into the seminary. MM. de Bernières, de Maizerets and Dudouyt vied in the imitation of their model, and they likewise abandoned to the holy house their goods and their pensions. The prelate confined himself, like the others, from humility even more than from economy on behalf of the community, to the greatest simplicity in dress as well as in his environment. Aiming at the highest degree of possible perfection, he was satisfied with the coarsest fare, and incessantly added voluntary privations to the sacrifices demanded of him by his difficult duties. Does not this apostolic poverty recall the seminary established by the pious founder of St. Sulpice, who wrote: "Each had at dinner a bowl of soup and a small portion of butcher's meat, without dessert, and in the evening likewise a little roast mutton"?

Mortification diminished in no wise the activity of the prelate; learning that the Seminary of Foreign Missions at Paris, that nursery of apostles, had just been definitely established (1663), he considered it his duty to establish his own more firmly by affiliating it with that of the French capital. "I have learned with joy," wrote he, "of the establishment of your Seminary of Foreign Missions, and that the gales and tempests by which it has been tossed since the beginning have but served to render it firmer and more unassailable. I cannot sufficiently praise your zeal, which, unable to confine itself to the limits and frontiers of France, seeks to spread throughout the world, and to pass beyond the seas into the most remote regions; considering which, I have thought I could not compass a greater good for our young Church, nor one more to the glory of God and the welfare of the peoples whom God has entrusted to our guidance, than by contributing to the establishment of one of your branches in Quebec, the place of our residence, where you will be like the light set upon the candlestick, to illumine all these regions by your holy doctrine and the example of your virtue. Since you are the torch of foreign countries, it is only reasonable that there should be no quarter of the globe uninfluenced by your charity and zeal. I hope that our Church will be one of the first to possess this good fortune, the more since it has already a part of what you hold most dear. Come then, and be welcome; we shall receive you with joy. You will find a lodging prepared and a fund sufficient to set up a small establishment, which I hope will continue to grow...." The act of union was signed in 1665, and was renewed ten years later with the royal assent.

Thanks to the generosity of Mgr. de Laval and of the first directors of the seminary, building and acquisition of land was begun. There was erected in 1668 a large wooden dwelling, which was in some sort an extension of the episcopal and parochial residence. It was destroyed in 1701, with the vicarage, in the conflagration which overwhelmed the whole seminary. Subsequently, there was purchased a site of sixteen acres adjoining the parochial church, upon which was erected the house of Madame Couillard. This house, in which lodged in 1668 the first pupils of the smaller seminary, was replaced in 1678 by a stone edifice, large enough to shelter all the pupils of both the seminaries. The seigniory of Beaupré was also acquired, which with remarkable foresight the bishop exchanged for the Ile Jésus. "It was prudent," remarks the Abbé Gosselin, "not to have all the property in the same place; when the seasons are bad in one part of the country they may be prosperous elsewhere; and having thus sources of revenue in different places, one is more likely never to find them entirely lacking."

The smaller seminary dates only from the year 1668. Up to this time the large seminary alone existed; of the five ecclesiastics who were its inmates in 1663, Louis Joliet abandoned the priestly career. It was he who, impelled by his adventurous instincts, sought out, together with Father Marquette, the mouth of the Mississippi.

[3] The house was first the presbytery.

CHAPTER V

MGR. DE LAVAL AND THE SAVAGES

Now, what were the results accomplished by the efforts of the missionaries at this period of our history? When in their latest hour they saw about them, as was very frequently the case, only the wild children of the desert uttering cries of ferocious joy, had they at least the consolation of discerning faithful disciples of Christ concealed among their executioners? Alas! we must admit that North America saw no renewal of the days when St. Peter converted on one occasion, at his first preaching, three thousand persons, and when St. Paul brought to Jesus by His word thousands of Gentiles. Were the missionaries of the New World, then, less zealous, less disinterested, less eloquent than the apostles of the early days of the Church? Let us listen to Mgr. Bourgard: "A few only among them, like the Brazilian apostle, Father Anthony Vieyra, died a natural death and found a grave in earth consecrated by the Church. Many, like Father Marquette, who reconnoitred the whole course of the Mississippi, succumbed to the burden of fatigue in the midst of the desert, and were buried under the turf by their sorrowful comrades. He had with him several Frenchmen, Fathers Badin, Deseille and Petit; the two latter left their venerable remains among the wastes. Others met death at the bedside of the plague-stricken, and were martyrs to their charity, like Fathers Turgis and Dablon. An incalculable number died in the desert, alone, deprived of all aid, unknown to the whole world, and their bodies became the sustenance of birds of prey. Several obtained the glorious crown of martyrdom; such are the venerable Fathers Jogues, Corpo, Souël, Chabanel, Ribourde,

Brébeuf, Lalemant, etc. Now they fell under the blows of raging Indians; now they were traitorously assassinated; again, they were impaled." In what, then, must we seek for the cause of the futility of these efforts? All those who know the savages will understand it; it is in the fickle character of these children of the woods, a character more unstable and volatile than that of infants. God alone knows what restless anxiety the conversions which they succeeded in bringing about caused to the missionaries and the pious Bishop of Petræa. Yet every day Mgr. de Laval ardently prayed, not only for the flock confided to his care but also for the souls which he had come from so far to seek to save from heathenism. If one of these devout men of God had succeeded at the price of a thousand dangers, of a thousand attempts, in proving to an Indian the insanity, the folly of his belief in the juggleries of a sorcerer, he must watch with jealous care lest his convert should lapse from grace either through the sarcasms of the other redskins, or through the attractions of some cannibal festival, or by the temptation to satisfy an ancient grudge, or through the fear of losing a coveted influence, or even through the apprehension of the vengeance of the heathen. Did he think himself justified in expecting to see his efforts crowned with success? Suddenly he would learn that the poor neophyte had been led astray by the sight of a bottle of brandy, and that he had to begin again from the beginning.

No greater success was attained in many efforts which were exerted to give a European stamp to the character of the aborigines, than in divers attempts to train in civilized habits young Indians brought up in the seminaries. And we know that if success in this direction had been possible it would certainly have been obtained by educators like the Jesuit Fathers. "With the French admitted to the small seminary," says the Abbé Ferland, "six young Indians were received; on the advice of the king they were all to be brought up together. This union, which was thought likely to prove useful to all, was not helpful to the savages, and became harmful to the young Frenchmen. After a few trials it was understood that it was impossible to adapt to the regular habits necessary for success in a course of study these young scholars who had been reared in complete freedom. Comradeship with Algonquin and Huron children, who were incapable of limiting themselves to the observance of a college rule, tended to give more force and persistence to the independent ideas which were natural in the young French-Canadians, who received from their fathers the love of liberty and the taste for an adventurous life."

But we must not infer, therefore, that the missionaries found no consolation in their troublous task. If sometimes the savage blood revealed itself in the neophytes in sudden insurrections, we must admit that the majority of the converts devoted themselves to the practice of virtues with an energy which often rose to heroism, and that already there began to appear among them that holy fraternity which the gospel everywhere brings to birth. The memoirs of the Jesuits furnish numerous evidences of this. We shall cite only the following: "A band of Hurons had come down to the Mission of St. Joseph. The Christians, suffering a great dearth of provisions, asked each other, 'Can we feed all those people?' As they said this, behold, a number of the Indians, disembarking from their little boats, go straight to the chapel, fall upon their knees and say their prayers. An Algonquin who had gone to salute the Holy Sacrament, having perceived them, came to apprise his captain that these Hurons were praying to God. 'Is it true?' said he. 'Come! come! we must no longer debate whether we shall give them food or not; they are our brothers, since they believe as well as we.'"

The conversion which caused the most joy to Mgr. de Laval was that of Garakontié, the noted chief of the Iroquois confederation. Accordingly he wished to baptize him himself in the cathedral of Quebec, and the governor, M. de Courcelles, consented to serve as godfather to the new follower of Christ. Up to this time the missions to the Five Nations had been ephemeral; by the first one Father Jogues had only been able to fertilize with his blood this barbarous soil; the second, established at Gannentaha, escaped the general massacre in 1658 only by a genuine miracle. This mission was commanded by Captain Dupuis, and comprised fifty-five Frenchmen. Five Jesuit Fathers were of the number, among them Fathers Chaumonot and Dablon. Everything up to that time had gone wonderfully well in the new establishment; the missionaries knew the Iroquois language so well, and so well applied the rules of savage eloquence, that they impressed all the surrounding tribes; accordingly they were full of trust and dreamed of a rapid extension of the Catholic faith in these territories. An Iroquois chief dispelled their illusion by revealing to them the plans of their enemies; they were already watched, and preparations were on foot to cut off their retreat. In this peril the colonists took counsel, and hastily constructed in the granaries of their quarters a few boats, some canoes and a large barge, destined to transport the provisions and the fugitives. They had to hasten, because the attack against their establishment might take place at any moment, and they must profit by the breaking up of the ice, which was impending. But how could they transport this little flotilla to the river which flowed into Lake Ontario twenty miles away without giving the alarm and being massacred at the first step? They adopted a singular stratagem derived from the customs of these people, and one in which the fugitives succeeded perfectly. "A young Frenchman adopted by an Indian," relates Jacques de Beaudoncourt, "pretended to have a dream by which he was warned to make a festival, 'to eat everything,' if he did not wish to die presently. 'You are my son,' replied the Iroquois chief, 'I do not want you to die; prepare the feast and we shall eat everything.' No one was absent; some of the French who were invited made music to charm the guests. They ate so much, according to the rules of Indian civility, that they said to their host, 'Take pity on us, and let us go and rest.' 'You want me to die, then?' 'Oh, no!' And they betook themselves to eating again as best they could. During this time the other Frenchmen were carrying to the river the boats and provisions. When all was ready the young man said: 'I take pity on you, stop eating, I shall not die. I am going to have music played to lull you to sleep.' And sleep was not long in coming, and the French, slipping hastily away from the banquet hall, rejoined their comrades. They had left the dogs and the fowls behind, in order the better to deceive the savages; a heavy snow, falling at the moment of their departure, had concealed all traces of their passage, and the banqueters imagined that a powerful Manitou had carried away the fugitives, who would not fail to come back and avenge themselves. After thirteen days of toilsome navigation, the French arrived in Montreal, having lost only three men from drowning during the passage. It had been thought that they were all massacred, for the plans of the Iroquois had become known in the colony; this escape brought the greatest honour to Captain Dupuis, who had successfully carried it out."

M. d'Argenson, then governor, did not approve of the retreat of the captain; this advanced bulwark protected the whole colony, and he thought that the French should have held out to the last man. This selfish opinion was disavowed by the great majority; the real courage of a leader does not consist in having all his comrades massacred to no purpose, but in saving by his calm intrepidity the largest possible number of soldiers for his country.

The Iroquois were tricked but not disarmed. Beside themselves with rage at the thought that so many victims about to be sacrificed to their hatred had escaped their blows, and desiring to end once for all the feud with their enemies, the Onondagas, they persuaded the other nations to join them in a rush upon Quebec. They succeeded easily, and twelve hundred savage warriors assembled at CleftRock, on the outskirts of Montreal, and exposed the colony to the most terrible danger which it had yet experienced.

This was indeed a great peril; the dwellings above Quebec were without defence, and separated so far from each other that they stretched out nearly two leagues. But providentially the plan of these terrible foes was made known to the inhabitants of the town through an Iroquois prisoner. Immediately the most feverish activity was exerted in preparations for defence; the country houses and those of the Lower Town were abandoned, and the inhabitants took refuge in the palace, in the fort, with the Ursulines, or with the Jesuits; redoubts were raised, loop-holes bored and patrols established. At Ville-Marie no fewer precautions were taken; the governor surrounded a mill which he had erected in 1658, by a palisade, a ditch, and four bastions well entrenched. It stood on a height of the St. Louis Hill, and, called at first the Mill on the Hill, it became later the citadel of Montreal. Anxiety still prevailed everywhere, but God, who knows how to raise up, in the very moment of despair, the instruments which He uses in His infinite wisdom to protect the countries dear to His heart, that same God who gave to France the heroic Joan of Arc, produced for Canada an unexpected defender. Dollard and sixteen brave Montrealers were to offer themselves as victims to save the colony. Their devotion, which surpasses all that history shows of splendid daring, proves the exaltation of the souls of those early colonists.

One morning in the month of July, 1660, Dollard, accompanied by sixteen valiant comrades, presented himself at the altar of the church in Montreal; these Christian heroes came to ask the God of the strong to bless the resolve which they had taken to go and sacrifice themselves for their brothers. Immediately after mass, tearing themselves from the embraces of their relatives, they set out, and after a long and toilsome march arrived at the foot of the Long Rapid, on the left bank of the Ottawa; the exact point where they stopped is probably Greece's Point, five or six miles above Carillon, for they knew that the Iroquois returning from the hunt must pass this place. They installed themselves within a wretched palisade, where they were joined almost at once by two Indian chiefs who, having challenged each other's courage, sought an occasion to surpass one another in valour. They were Anahotaha, at the head of forty Hurons, and Métiomègue, accompanied by four Algonquins. They had not long to wait; two canoes bore the Iroquois crews within musket shot; those who escaped the terrible volley which received them and killed the majority of them, hastened to warn the band of three hundred other Iroquois from whom they had become detached. The Indians, relying on an easy victory, hastened up, but they hurled themselves in vain upon the French, who, sheltered by their weak palisade, crowned its stakes with the heads of their enemies as these were beaten down. Exasperated by this unexpected check, the Iroquois broke up the canoes of their adversaries, and, with the help of these fragments, which they set on fire, attempted to burn the little fortress; but a well sustained fire prevented the rashest from approaching. Their pride yielding to their thirst for vengeance, these three hundred men found themselves too few before such intrepid enemies, and they sent for aid to a band of five hundred of their people, who were camped on the Richelieu Islands. These hastened to the attack, and eight hundred men rushed upon a band of heroes strengthened by the sentiment of duty, the love of country and faith in a happy future. Futile efforts! The bullets made terrible havoc in their ranks, and they recoiled again, carrying with them only the assurance that their numbers had not paralyzed the courage of the French.

But the aspect of things was about to change, owing to the cowardice of the Hurons. Water failed the besieged tortured by thirst; they made sorties from time to time to procure some, and could bring back in their small and insufficient vessels only a few drops, obtained at the greatest peril. The Iroquois, aware of this fact, profited by it in order to offer life and pardon to the Indians who would go over to their side. No more was necessary to persuade the Hurons, and suddenly thirty of them followed La Mouche, the nephew of the Huron chief, and leaped over the palisades. The brave Anahotaha fired a pistol shot at his nephew, but missed him. The Algonquins remained faithful, and died bravely at their post. The Iroquois learned through these deserters the real number of those who were resisting them so boldly; they then took an oath to die to the last man rather than renounce victory, rather than cast thus an everlasting opprobrium on their nation. The bravest made a sort of shield with fagots tied together, and, placing themselves in front of their comrades, hurled themselves upon the palisades, attempting to tear them up. The supreme moment of the struggle has come; Dollard is aware of it. While his brothers in arms make frightful gaps in the ranks of the savages by well-directed shots, he loads with grape shot a musket which is to explode as it falls, and hurls it with all his might. Unhappily, the branch of a tree stays the passage of the terrible engine of destruction, which falls back upon the French and makes a bloody gap among them. "Surrender!" cries La Mouche to Anahotaha. "I have given my word to the French, I shall die with them," replies the bold chief. Already some stakes were torn up, and the Iroquois were about to rush like an avalanche through this breach, when a new Horatius Cocles, as brave as the Roman, made his body a shield for his brothers, and soon the axe which he held in his hand dripped with blood. He fell, and was at once replaced. The French succumbed one by one; they were seen brandishing their weapons up to the moment of their last breath, and, riddled with wounds, they resisted to the last sigh.

Drunk with vengeance, the wild conquerors turned over the bodies to find some still palpitating, that they might bind them to a stake of torture; three were in their mortal agony, but they died before being cast on the pyre. A single one was saved for the stake; he heroically resisted the refinements of the most barbarous cruelty; he showed no weakness, and did not cease to pray for his executioners. Everything in this glorious deed of arms must compel the admiration of the most remote posterity.

The wretched Hurons suffered the fate which they had deserved; they were burned in the different villages. Five escaped, and it was by their reports that men learned the details of an exploit which saved the colony. The Iroquois, in fact, considering what a handful of brave men had accomplished, took it for granted that a frontal attack on such men could only result in failure; they changed their tactics, and had recourse anew to their warfare of surprises and ambuscades, with the purpose of gradually destroying the little colony.

The dangers which might be risked by attacking so fierce a nation were, as may be seen, by no means imaginary. Many would have retreated, and awaited a favourable occasion to try and plant for the third time the cross in the Iroquois village. The sons of Loyola did not hesitate; encouraged by Mgr. de Laval, they retraced their steps to the Five Nations. This time Heaven condescended to reward in a large measure their persistent efforts, and the harvest was abundant. In a short time the number of churches among these people had increased to ten.

The famous chief, Garakontié, whose conversion to Christianity caused so much joy to the pious Bishop of Petræa and to all the Christians of Canada, was endowed with a rare intelligence, and all who approached him recognized in him a mind as keen as it was profound. Not only did he keep faithfully the promises which he had made on receiving baptism, but the gratitude which he continued to feel towards the bishop and the missionaries made him remain until his death the devoted friend of the French. "He is an incomparable man," wrote Father Millet one day. "He is the soul of all the good that is done here; he supports the faith by his influence; he maintains peace by his authority; he declares himself so clearly for France that we may justly call him the protector of the Crown in this country." Feeling life escaping, he wished to give what the savages call their "farewell feast," a touching custom, especially when Christianity comes to sanctify it. His last words were for the venerable prelate, to whom he had vowed a deep attachment and respect. "The guests having retired," wrote Father Lamberville, "he called me to him. 'So we must part at last,' said he to me; 'I am willing, since I hope to go to Heaven.' He then begged me to tell my beads with him, which I did, together with several Christians, and then he called me and said to me: 'I am dying.' Then he gave up the ghost very peacefully."

The labour demanded at this period by pastoral visits in a diocese so extended may readily be imagined. Besides the towns of Quebec, Montreal and Three Rivers, in which was centralized the general activity, there were then several Christian villages, those of Lorette, Ste. Foy, Sillery, the village of La Montagne at Montreal, of the Sault St. Louis, and of the Prairie de la Madeleine. Far from avoiding these trips, Mgr. de Laval took pleasure in visiting all the cabins of the savages, one after another, spreading the good Word, consoling the afflicted, and himself administering the sacraments of the Church to those who wished to receive them.

Father Dablon gives us in these terms the narrative of the visit of the bishop to the Prairie de la Madeleine in 1676. "This man," says he, speaking of the prelate, "this man, great by birth and still greater by his virtues, which have been quite recently the admiration of all France, and which on his last voyage to Europe justly acquired for him the esteem and the approval of the king; this great man, making the rounds of his diocese, was conveyed in a little bark canoe by two peasants, exposed to all the inclemencies of the climate, without other retinue than a single ecclesiastic, and without carrying anything but a wooden cross and the ornaments absolutely necessary to a *bishop of gold*, according to the expression of authors in speaking of the first prelates of Christianity."

[The expedition of Dollard is related in detail by Dollier de Casson, and by Mother Mary of the Incarnation in her letters. The Abbé de Belmont gives a further account of the episode in his history. The *Jesuit Relations* place the scene of the affair at the Chaudière Falls. The sceptically-minded are referred to Kingsford's *History of Canada*, vol. I., p. 261, where a less romantic view of the affair is taken.]—Editors' Note on the Dollard Episode.

CHAPTER VI

SETTLEMENT OF THE COLONY

To the great joy of Mgr. de Laval the colony was about to develop suddenly, thanks to the establishment in the fertile plains of New France of the time-expired soldiers of the regiment of Carignan. The importance of the peopling of his diocese had always been capital in the eyes of the bishop, and we have seen him at work obtaining from the court new consignments of colonists. Accordingly, in the year 1663, three hundred persons had embarked at La Rochelle for Canada. Unfortunately, the majority of these passengers were quite young people, clerks or students, in quest of adventure, who had never worked with their hands. The consequences of this deplorable emigration were disastrous; more than sixty of these poor children died during the voyage. The king was startled at such negligence, and the three hundred colonists who embarked the following year, in small detachments, arrived in excellent condition. Moreover, they had made the voyage without expense, but had in return hired to work for three years with the farmers, for an annual wage which was to be fixed by the authorities. "It will seem to you perhaps strange," wrote M. de Villeray, to the minister Colbert, "to see that we make workmen coming to us from France undergo a sort of apprenticeship, by distribution among the inhabitants; yet there is nothing more necessary, first, because the men brought to us are not accustomed to the tilling of the soil; secondly, a man who is not accustomed to work, unless he is urged, has difficulty in adapting himself to it; thirdly, the tasks of this country are very different from those of France, and experience shows us that a man who has wintered three years in the country, and who then hires out at service, receives double the wages of one just arriving from the Old Country. These are reasons of our own which possibly would not be admitted in France by those who do not understand them."

The Sovereign Council recommended, moreover, that there should be sent only men from the north of France, "because," it asserted, "the Normans, Percherons, Picards, and people from the neighbourhood of Paris are docile, laborious, industrious, and have much more religion. Now, it is important in the establishment of a country to sow good seed." While we accept in the proper spirit this eulogy of our ancestors, who came mostly from these provinces, how inevitably it suggests a comparison with the spirit of scepticism and irreverence which now infects, transitorily, let us hope, these regions of Northern France.

Never before had the harbour of Quebec seen so much animation as in the year 1665. The solicitor-general, Bourdon, had set foot on the banks of the St. Lawrence in early spring; he escorted a number of girls chosen by order of the queen. Towards the middle of August two ships arrived bearing four companies of the regiment of Carignan, and the following month three other vessels brought, together with eight other companies, Governor de Courcelles and Commissioner Talon. Finally, on October 2nd, one hundred and thirty robust colonists and eighty-two maidens, carefully chosen, came to settle in the colony.

If we remember that there were only at this time seventy houses in Quebec, we may say without exaggeration that the number of persons who came from France in this year, 1665, exceeded that of the whole white population already resident in Canada. But it was desirable to keep this population in its entirety, and Commissioner Talon, well seconded by Mgr. de Laval, tenaciously pursued this purpose. The soldiers of Carignan, all brave, and pious too, for the most part, were highly desirable colonists. "What we seek most," wrote Mother Mary of the Incarnation, "is the glory of God and the welfare of souls. That is what we are working for, as well as to assure the prevalence of devotion in the army, giving the men to understand that we are waging here a holy war. There are as many as five hundred of them who have taken the scapulary of the Holy Virgin, and many others who recite the chaplet of the Holy Family every day."

Talon met with a rather strong opposition to his immigration plans in the person of the great Colbert, who was afraid of seeing the Mother Country depopulated in favour of her new daughter Canada. His perseverance finally won the day, and more than four hundred soldiers settled in the colony. Each common soldier received a hundred francs, each sergeant a hundred and fifty francs. Besides, forty thousand francs were used in raising in France the additional number of fifty girls and a hundred and fifty men, which, increased by two hundred and thirty-five colonists, sent by the company in 1667, fulfilled the desires of the Bishop of Petræa.

The country would soon have been self-supporting if similar energy had been continuously employed in its development. It is a miracle that a handful of emigrants, cast almost without resources upon the northern shore of America, should have been able to maintain themselves so long, in spite of continual alarms, in spite of the deprivation of all comfort, and in spite of the rigour of the climate. With wonderful courage and patience they conquered a vast territory, peopled it, cultivated its soil, and defended it by prodigies of valour against the forays of the Indians.

The colony, happily, was to keep its bishop, the worthy Governor de Courcelles, and the best administrator it ever had, the Commissioner Talon. But it was to lose a lofty intellect: the Marquis de Tracy, his mission ended to the satisfaction of all, set sail again for France. From the moment of his arrival in Canada the latter had inspired the greatest confidence. "These three gentlemen," say the annals of the hospital, speaking of the viceroy, of M. de Courcelles and M. Talon, "were endowed with all desirable qualities. They added to an attractive exterior much wit, gentleness and prudence, and were admirably adapted to instil a high idea of the royal majesty and power; they sought all means proper for moulding the country and laboured at this task with great application. This colony, under their wise leadership, expanded wonderfully, and according to all appearances gave hope of becoming most flourishing." Mgr. de Laval held the Marquis de Tracy in high esteem. "He is a man powerful in word and deed," he wrote to Pope Alexander VII, "a practising Christian, and the right arm of religion." The viceroy did not fear, indeed, to show that one may be at once an excellent Christian and a brave officer, whether he accompanied the Bishop of Petræa on the pilgrimage to good Ste. Anne, or whether he honoured himself in the religious processions by carrying a corner of the daïs with the governor, the intendant and the agent of the West India Company. He was seen also at the laying of the foundation stone of the church of the Jesuits, at the transfer of the relics of the holy martyrs Flavian and Felicitas, at the consecration of the cathedral of Quebec and at that of the chief altar of the church of the Ursulines, in fact, everywhere where he might set before the faithful the good example of piety and of the respect due to religion.

The eighteen years of peace with the Iroquois, obtained by the expedition of the Marquis de Tracy, allowed the intendant to encourage the development of the St. Maurice mines, to send the traveller Nicolas Perrot to visit all the tribes of the north and west, in order to establish or cement with them relations of trade or friendship, and to entrust Father Marquette and M. Joliet with the mission of exploring the course of the Mississippi. The two travellers carried their exploration as far as the junction of this river with the Arkansas, but their provisions failing them, they had to retrace their steps.

This state of peace came near being disturbed by the gross cupidity of some wretched soldiers. In the spring of 1669 three soldiers of the garrison of Ville-Marie, intoxicated and assassinated an Iroquois chief who was bringing back from his hunting some magnificent furs. M. de Courcelles betook himself at once to Montreal, but, during the process of this trial, it was learned that several months before three other Frenchmen had killed six Mohegan Indians with the same purpose of plunder. The excitement aroused by these two murders was such that a general uprising of the savage nations was feared; already they had banded together for vengeance, and only the energy of the governor saved the colony from the horrors of another war. In the presence of all the Indians then quartered at Ville-Marie, he had the three assassins of the Iroquois chief brought before him, and caused them to be shot. He pledged himself at the same time to do like justice to the murderers of the Mohegans, as soon as they should be discovered. He caused, moreover, to be restored to the widow of the chief all the furs which had been stolen from him, and indemnified the two tribes, and thus by his firmness induced the restless nations to remain at peace. His vigilance did not stop at this. The Iroquois and the Ottawas being on the point of recommencing their feud, he warned them that he would not allow them to disturb the general order and tranquillity. He commanded them to send to him delegates to present the question of their mutual grievances. Receiving an arrogant reply from the Iroquois, who thought their country inaccessible to the French, he himself set out from Montreal on June 2nd, 1671, with fifty-six soldiers, in a specially constructed boat and thirteen bark canoes. He reached the entrance to Lake Ontario, and so daunted the Iroquois by his audacity that the Ottawas sued for peace. Profiting by the alarm with which he had just inspired them, M.de Courcelles gave orders to the principal chiefs to go and await him at Cataraqui, there to treat with him on an important matter. They obeyed, and the governor declared to them his plan of constructing at this very place a fort where they might more easily arrange their exchanges. Not suspecting that the French had any other purpose than that of protecting themselves against inroads, they approved this plan; and so Fort Cataraqui, to-day the city of Kingston, was erected by Count de Frontenac, and called after this governor, who was to succeed M. de Courcelles.

Their transitory apprehensions did not interrupt the construction of the two churches of Quebec and Montreal, for they were built almost at the same time; the first was dedicated on July 11th, 1666, the second, begun in 1672, was finished only in 1678. The church of the old city of Champlain was of stone, in the form of a Roman cross; its length was one hundred feet, its width thirty-eight. It contained, besides the principal altar, a chapel dedicated to St. Joseph, another to Ste. Anne, and the chapel of the Holy Scapulary. Thrice enlarged, it gave place in 1755 to the present cathedral, for which the foundations of the older church were used. When the prelate arrived in 1659, the holy offices were already celebrated there, but the bishop hastened to end the work which it still required. "There is here," he wrote to the Common Father of the faithful, "a cathedral made of stone; it is large and splendid. The divine service is celebrated in it according to the ceremony of bishops; our priests, our seminarists, as well as ten or twelve choir-boys, are regularly present there. On great festivals, the mass, vespers and evensong are sung to music, with orchestral accompaniment, and our organs mingle their harmonious voices with those of the chanters. There are in the sacristy some very fine ornaments, eight silver chandeliers, and all the chalices, pyxes, vases and censers are either gilt or pure silver."

The Sulpicians as well as the Jesuits have always professed a peculiar devotion to the Virgin Mary. It was the pious founder of St. Sulpice, M. Olier, who suggested to the Company of Notre-Dame the idea of consecrating to Mary the establishment of the Island of Montreal in order that she might defend it as her property, and increase it as her domain. They gladly yielded to this desire, and even adopted as the seal of the company the figure of Our Lady; in addition they confirmed the name of Ville-Marie, so happily given to this chosen soil.

It was the Jesuits who placed the church of Quebec under the patronage of the Immaculate Conception, and gave it as second patron St. Louis, King of France. This double choice could not but be agreeable to the pious Bishop of Petræa. Learning, moreover, that the members of the Society of Jesus renewed each year in Canada their vow to fast on the eve of the festival of the Immaculate Conception, and to add to this mortification several pious practices, with the view of obtaining from Heaven the conversion of the savages, he approved this devotion, and ordered that in future it should likewise be observed in his seminary. He sanctioned other works of piety inspired or established by the Jesuit Fathers; the *novena*, which has remained so popular with the French-Canadians, at St. François-Xavier, the Brotherhoods of the Holy Rosary and of the Scapulary of Our Lady of Mount Carmel. He encouraged, above all, devotion to the Holy Family, and prescribed wise regulations for this worship. The Pope deigned to enrich by numerous indulgences the brotherhoods to which it gave birth, and in recent years Leo XIII instituted throughout the Church the celebration of the Festival of the Holy Family. "The worship of the Holy Family," the illustrious pontiff proclaims in a recent bull, "was established in America, in the region of Canada, where it became most flourishing, thanks chiefly to the solicitude and activity of the venerable servant of God, François de Montmorency Laval, first Bishop of Quebec, and of God's worthy handmaiden, Marguerite Bourgeoys." According to Cardinal

Taschereau, it was Father Pijard who established the first Brotherhood of the Holy Family in 1650 in the Island of Montreal, but the real promoter of this cult was another Father of the Company of Jesus, Father Chaumonot, whom Mgr. de Laval brought specially to Quebec to set at the head of the brotherhood which he had decided to found.

It was the custom, in these periods of fervent faith, to place buildings, cities and even countries under the ægis of a great saint, and Louis XIII had done himself the honour of dedicating France to the Virgin Mary. People did not then blush to practise and profess their beliefs, nor to proclaim them aloud. On the proposal of the Récollets in a general assembly, St. Joseph was chosen as the first patron saint of Canada; later, St. François-Xavier was adopted as the second special protector of the colony.

Montreal, which in the early days of its existence maintained with its rival of Cape Diamond a strife of emulation in the path of good as well as in that of progress, could no longer do without a religious edifice worthy of its already considerable importance. Mgr. de Laval was at this time on a round of pastoral visits, for, in spite of the fatigue attaching to such a journey, at a time when there was not yet even a carriage-road between the two towns, and when, braving contrary winds, storms and the snares of the Iroquois, one had to ascend the St. Lawrence in a bark canoe, the worthy prelate made at least eight visits to Montreal during the period of his administration. In a general assembly of May 12th, 1669, presided over by him, it was decided to establish the church on ground which had belonged to Jean de Saint-Père, but since this site had not the elevation on which the Sulpicians desired to see the new temple erected, the work was suspended for two years more. The ecclesiastics of the seminary offered on this very height (for M. Dollier had given to the main street the name of Notre-Dame, which was that of the future church) some lots bought by them from Nicolas Godé and from Mme. Jacques Lemoyne, and situated behind their house; they offered besides in the name of M. de Bretonvilliers the sum of a thousand *livres tournois* for three years, to begin the work. These offers were accepted in an assembly of all the inhabitants, on June 10th, 1672; François Bailly, master mason, directed the building, and on the thirtieth of the same month, before the deeply moved and pious population, there were laid, immediately after high mass, the first five stones. There had been chosen the name of the Purification, because this day was the anniversary of that on which MM. Olier and de la Dauversière had caught the first glimpses of their vocation to work at the establishment of Ville-Marie, and because this festival had always remained in high honour among the Montrealers. The foundation was laid by M. de Courcelles, governor-general; the second stone had been reserved for M. Talon, but, as he could not accept the invitation, his place was taken by M. Philippe de Carion, representative of M. de la Motte Saint-Paul. The remaining stones were laid by M. Perrot, governor of the island, by M. Dollier de Casson, representing M. de Bretonvilliers, and by Mlle. Mance, foundress of the Montreal hospital. The sight of this ceremony was one of the last joys of this good woman; she died on June 18th of the following year.

Meanwhile, all desired to contribute to the continuation of the work; some offered money, others materials, still others their labour. In their ardour the priests of the seminary had the old fort, which was falling into ruins, demolished in order to use the wood and stone for the new building. As lords of the island, they seemed to have the incontestable right to dispose of an edifice which was their private property. But M. de Bretonvilliers, to whom they referred the matter, took them to task for their haste, and according to his instructions the work of demolition was stopped, not to be resumed until ten years later. The colonists had an ardent desire to see their church finished, but they were poor, and, though a collection had brought in, in 1676, the sum of two thousand seven hundred francs, the work dragged along for two years more, and was finished only in 1678. "The church had," says M. Morin, "the form of a Roman cross, with the lower sides ending in a circular apse; its portal, built of hewn stone, was composed of two designs, one Tuscan, the other Doric; the latter was surmounted by a triangular pediment. This beautiful entrance, erected in 1722, according to the plans of= Chaussegros de Léry, royal engineer, was flanked on the right side by a square tower crowned by a campanile, from the summit of which rose a beautiful cross with *fleur-de-lis* twenty-four feet high. This church was built in the axis of Notre-Dame Street, and a portion of it on the Place d'Armes; it measured, in the clear, one hundred and forty feet long, and ninety-six feet wide, and the tower one hundred and forty-four feet high. It was razed in 1830, and the tower demolished in 1843."

Montreal continued to progress, and therefore to build. The Sulpicians, finding themselves cramped in their old abode, began in 1684 the construction of a new seigniorial and chapter house, of one hundred and seventy-eight feet frontage by eighty-four feet deep. These vast buildings, whose main façade faces on Notre-Dame Street, in front of the Place d'Armes, still exist. They deserve the attention of the tourist, if only by reason of their antiquity, and on account of the old clock which surmounts them, for though it is the most ancient of all in North America, this clock still marks the hours with average exactness. Behind these old walls extends a magnificent garden.

The spectacle presented by Ville-Marie at this time was most edifying. This great village was the school of martyrdom, and all aspired thereto, from the most humble artisan and the meanest soldier to the brigadier, the commandant, the governor, the priests and the nuns, and they found in this aspiration, this faith and this hope, a strength and happiness known only to the chosen. From the bosom of this city had sprung the seventeen heroes who gave to the world, at the foot of the Long Sault, a magnificent example of what the spirit of Christian sacrifice can do; to a population which gave of its own free will its time and its labour to the building of a temple for the Lord, God had assigned a leader, who took upon his shoulders a heavy wooden cross, and bore it for the distance of a league up the steep flanks of Mount Royal, to plant it solemnly upon the summit; within the walls of the seminary lived men like M. Souart, physician of hearts and bodies, or like MM. Lemaître and Vignal, who were destined to martyrdom; in the halls of the hospital Mlle. Mance vied with Sisters de Brésoles, Maillet and de Macé, in attending to the most repugnant infirmities or healing the most tedious maladies; last but not least, Sister Bourgeoys and her pious comrades, Sisters

Aimée Chatel, Catherine Crolo, and Marie Raisin, who formed the nucleus of the Congregation, devoted themselves with unremitting zeal to the arduous task of instruction.

Another favour was about to be vouchsafed to Canada in the birth of Mlle. Leber. M. de Maisonneuve and Mlle. Mance were her godparents, and the latter gave her her baptismal name. Jeanne Leber reproduced all the virtues of her godmother, and gave to Canada an example worthy of the primitive Church, and such as finds small favour in the practical world of to-day. She lived a recluse for twenty years with the Sisters of the Congregation, and practised, till death relieved her, mortifications most terrifying to the physical nature.

At Quebec, the barometer of piety, if I may be excused so bold a metaphor, held at the same level as that of Montreal, and he would be greatly deceived who, having read only the history of the early years of the latter city, should despair of finding in the centre of edification founded by Champlain, men worthy to rank with Queylus and Lemaître, with Souart and Vignal, with Closse and Maisonneuve, and women who might vie with Marguerite Bourgeoys, with Jeanne Mance or with Jeanne Leber. To the piety of the Sulpicians of the colony planted at the foot of Mount Royal corresponded the fervour both of the priests who lived under the same roof as Mgr. de Laval, and of the sons of Loyola, who awaited in their house at Quebec their chance of martyrdom; the edifying examples given by the military chiefs of Montreal were equalled by those set by governors like de Mézy and de Courcelles; finally the virtues bordering on perfection of women like Mlle. Leber and the foundresses of the hospital and the Congregation found their equivalents in those of the pious Bishop of Petræa, of Mme. de la Peltrie and those of Mothers Mary of the Incarnation and Andrée Duplessis de Sainte-Hélène.

The Church will one day, perhaps, set upon her altars Mother Mary of the Incarnation, the first superior of the Ursulines at Quebec. The Theresa of New France, as she has been called, was endowed with a calm courage, an incredible patience, and a superior intellect, especially in spiritual matters; we find the proof of this in her letters and meditations which her son published in France. "At the head," says the Abbé Ferland, "of a community of weak women, devoid of resources, she managed to inspire her companions with the strength of soul and the trust in God which animated herself. In spite of the unteachableness and the fickleness of the Algonquin maidens, the troublesome curiosity of their parents, the thousand trials of a new and poor establishment, Mother Incarnation preserved an evenness of temper which inspired her comrades in toil with courage. Did some sudden misfortune appear, she arose with all the greatness of a Christian of the primitive Church to meet it with steadfastness. If her son spoke to her of the ill-treatment to which she was exposed on the part of the Iroquois, at a time when the affairs of the French seemed desperate, she replied calmly: 'Have no anxiety for me. I do not speak as to martyrdom, for your affection for me would incline you to desire it for me, but I mean as to other outrages. I see no reason for apprehension; all that I hear does not dismay me.' When she was cast out upon the snow, together with her sisters, in the middle of a winter's night, by reason of a conflagration which devoured her convent, her first act was to prevail upon her companions to kneel with her to thank God for having preserved their lives, though He despoiled them of all that they possessed in the world. Her strong and noble soul seemed to rise naturally above the misfortunes which assailed the growing colony. Trusting fully to God through the most violent storms, she continued to busy herself calmly with her work, as if nothing in the world had been able to move her. At a moment when many feared that the French would be forced to leave the country, Mother of the Incarnation, in spite of her advanced age, began to study the language of the Hurons in order to make herself useful to the young girls of this tribe. Ever tranquil, she did not allow herself to be carried away by enthusiasm or stayed by fear. 'We imagine sometimes,' she wrote to her former superior at Tours, 'that a certain passing inclination is a vocation; no, events show the contrary. In our momentary enthusiasms we think more of ourselves than of the object we face, and so we see that when this enthusiasm is once past, our tendencies and inclinations remain on the ordinary plane of life.' Built on such a foundation, her piety was solid, sincere and truly enlightened. In perusing her writings, we are astonished at finding in them a clearness of thought, a correctness of style, and a firmness of judgment which give us a lofty idea of this really superior woman. Clever in handling the brush as well as the pen, capable of directing the work of building as well as domestic labour, she combined, according to the opinion of her contemporaries, all the qualities of the strong woman of whom the Holy Scriptures give us so fine a portrait. She was entrusted with all the business of the convent. She wrote a prodigious number of letters, she learned the two mother tongues of the country, the Algonquin and the Huron, and composed for the use of her sisters, a sacred history in Algonquin, a catechism in Huron, an Iroquois catechism and dictionary, and a dictionary, catechism and collection of prayers in the Algonquin language."

CHAPTER VII

THE SMALLER SEMINARY

The smaller seminary, founded by the Bishop of Petræa in 1668, for youths destined to the ecclesiastical life, justified the expectations of its founder, and witnessed an ever increasing influx of students. On the day of its inauguration, October 9th, there were only as yet eight French pupils and six Huron children. For lack of teachers the young neophytes, placed under the guidance of directors connected with the seminary, attended during the first years the classes of the Jesuit Fathers. Their special costume was a blue cloak, confined by a belt. At this period the College of the Jesuits contained already some sixty resident scholars, and what proves to us that serious studies were here pursued is that several scholars are quoted in the memoirs as having successfully defended in the presence of the highest authorities of the colony theses on physics and philosophy.

If the first bishop of New France had confined himself to creating one large seminary, it is certain that his chosen work, which was the preparation for the Church of a nursery of scholars and priests, the apostles of the future, would not have been complete.

For many young people, indeed, who lead a worldly existence, and find themselves all at once transferred to the serious, religious life of the seminary, the surprise, and sometimes the discomfort, may be great. One must adapt oneself to this atmosphere of prayer, meditation and study. The rules of prayer are certainly not beyond the limits of an ordinary mind, but the practice is more difficult than the theory. Not without effort can a youthful imagination, a mind ardent and consumed by its own fervour, relinquish all the memories of family and social occupations, in order to withdraw into silence, inward peace, and the mortification of the senses. To the devoutly-minded our worldly life may well seem petty in comparison with the more spiritual existence, and in the religious life, for the priest especially, lies the sole source and the indispensable condition of happiness. But one must learn to be thus happy by humility, study and prayer, as one learns to be a soldier by obedience, discipline and exercise, and in nothing did Laval more reveal his discernment than in the recognition of the fact that the transition from one life to the other must be effected only after careful instruction and wisely-guided deliberation.

The aim of the smaller seminary is to guide, by insensible gradations towards the great duties and the great responsibilities of the priesthood, young men upon whom the spirit of God seems to have rested. There were in Israel schools of prophets; this does not mean that their training ended in the diploma of a seer or an oracle, but that this novitiate was favourable to the action of God upon their souls, and inclined them thereto. A smaller seminary possesses also the hope of the harvest. It is there that the minds of the students, by exercises proportionate to their age, become adapted unconstrainedly to pious reading, to the meditation and the grave studies in whose cycle the life of the priest must pass.

We shall not be surprised if the prelate's followers recognized in the works of faith which sprang up in his footsteps and progressed on all hands at Ville-Marie and at Quebec shining evidences of the protection of Mary to whose tutelage they had dedicated their establishments. This protection indeed has never been withheld, since to-day the fame of the university which sprang from the seminary, as a fruit develops from a bud, has crossed the seas. Father Monsabré, the eloquent preacher of Notre-Dame in Paris, speaking of the union of science and faith, exclaimed: "There exists, in the field of the New World, an institution which has religiously preserved this holy alliance and the traditions of the older universities, the Laval University of Quebec."

Mgr. de Laval, while busying himself with the training of his clergy, watched over the instruction of youth. He protected his schools and his dioceses; at Quebec the Jesuits, and later the seminary, maintained even elementary schools. If we must believe the Abbé de Latour and other writers of the seventeenth and eighteenth centuries, the children of the early colonists, skilful in manual labour, showed, nevertheless, great indolence of mind. "In general," writes Latour, "Canadian children have intelligence, memory and facility, and they make rapid progress, but the fickleness of their character, a dominant taste for liberty, and their hereditary and natural inclination for physical exercise do not permit them to apply themselves with sufficient perseverance and assiduity to become learned men; satisfied with a certain measure of knowledge sufficient for the ordinary purposes of their occupations (and this is, indeed, usually possessed), we see no people deeply learned in any branch of science. We must further admit that there are few resources, few books, and little emulation. No doubt the resources will be multiplied, and clever persons will appear in proportion as the colony increases." Always eager to develop all that might serve for the propagation of the faith or the progress of the colony, the devoted prelate eagerly fostered this natural aptitude of the Canadians for the arts and trades, and he established at St. Joachim a boarding-school for country children; this offered, besides a solid primary education, lessons in agriculture and some training for different trades.

Mgr. de Laval gave many other proofs of his enlightened charity for the poor and the waifs of fortune; he approved and encouraged among other works the Brotherhood of Saint Anne at Quebec. This association of prayer and spiritual aid had been established but three years before his arrival; it was directed by a chaplain and two directors, the latter elected annually by secret ballot. He had wished to offer in 1660 a more striking proof of his devotion to the Mother of the Holy Virgin, and had caused to be built on the shore of Beaupré the first sanctuary of Saint Anne. This temple arose not far from a chapel begun two years before, under the care of the Abbé de Queylus. The origin of this place of devotion, it appears, was a great peril to which certain Breton sailors were exposed: assailed by a tempest in the Gulf of St. Lawrence, about the beginning of the seventeenth century, they made a vow to erect, if they escaped death, a chapel to good Saint Anne on the spot where they should land. Heaven heard their prayers, and they kept their word. The chapel erected by Mgr. de Laval was a very modest one, but the zealous missionary of Beaupré, the Abbé Morel, then chaplain, was the witness of many acts of ardent faith and sincere piety; the Bishop of Petræa himself made several pilgrimages to the place. "We confess," says he, "that nothing has aided us more efficaciously to support the burden of the pastoral charge of this growing church than the special devotion which all the inhabitants of this country dedicate to Saint Anne, a devotion which, we affirm it with certainty, distinguishes them from all other peoples." The poor little chapel, built of uprights, gave place in 1675 to a stone church erected by the efforts of M. Filion, proctor of the seminary, and it was noted for an admirable picture given by the viceroy, de Tracy, who did not disdain to make his pilgrimage like the rest, and to set thus an example which the great ones of the earth should more frequently give. This church lasted only a few years; Mgr. de Laval was still living when a third temple was built upon its site. This was enlarged in 1787, and gave place only in 1878 to the magnificent cathedral which we admire to-day. The faith which raised this sanctuary to consecrate it to Saint Anne did not die with its pious founder; it is still lively in our hearts, since in 1898 a hundred and twenty thousand pilgrims went to pray before the relic of Saint Anne, the precious gift of Mgr. de Laval.

In our days, hardly has the sun melted the thick mantle of snow which covers during six months the Canadian soil, hardly has the majestic St. Lawrence carried its last blocks of ice down to the ocean, when caravans of pious pilgrims from all quarters of the country wend their way towards the sanctuary raised upon the shores of Beaupré. Whole families fill the cars; the boats of the Richelieu Company stop to receive passengers at all the charming villages strewn along the banks of the river, and the cathedral which raises in the air its slender spires on either side of the immense statue of Saint Anne does not suffice to contain the ever renewed throng of the faithful.

Even in the time of Mgr. de Laval, pilgrimages to Saint Anne's were frequent, and it was not only French people but also savages who addressed to the Mother of the Virgin Mary fervent, and often very artless, prayers. The harvest became, in fact, more abundant in the missions, and

"Les prêtres ne pouvaient suffire aux sacrifices."[4]

From the banks of the Saguenay at Tadousac, or from the shore of Hudson Bay, where Father Albanel was evangelizing the Indians, to the recesses of the Iroquois country, a Black Robe taught from interval to interval in a humble chapel the truths of the Christian religion. "We may say," wrote Father Dablon in 1671, "that the torch of the faith now illumines the four quarters of this New World. More than seven hundred baptisms have this year consecrated all our forests; more than twenty different missions incessantly occupy our Fathers among more than twenty diverse nations; and the chapels erected in the districts most remote from here are almost every day filled with these poor barbarians, and in some of them there have been consummated sometimes ten, twenty, and even thirty baptisms on a single occasion." And, ever faithful to the established power, the missionaries taught their neophytes not only religion, but also the respect due to the king. Let us hearken to Father Allouez speaking to the mission of Sault Ste. Marie: "Cast your eyes," says he, "upon the cross raised so high above your heads. It was upon that cross that Jesus Christ, the son of God, become a man by reason of His love for men, consented to be bound and to die, in order to satisfy His Eternal Father for our sins. He is the master of our life, the master of Heaven, earth and hell. It is He of whom I speak to you without ceasing, and whose name and word I have borne into all these countries. But behold at the same time this other stake, on which are hung the arms of the great captain of France, whom we call the king. This great leader lives beyond the seas; he is the captain of the greatest captains, and has not his peer in the world. All the captains that you have ever seen, and of whom you have heard speak, are only children beside him. He is like a great tree; the rest are only little plants crushed under men's footsteps as they walk. You know Onontio, the famous chieftain of Quebec; you know that he is the terror of the Iroquois, his mere name makes them tremble since he has desolated their country and burned their villages. Well, there are beyond the seas ten thousand Onontios like him. They are only the soldiers of this great captain, our great king, of whom I speak to you."

Mgr. de Laval ardently desired, then, the arrival of new workers for the gospel, and in the year 1668, the very year of the foundation of the seminary, his desire was fulfilled, as if Providence wished to reward His servant at once. Missionaries from France came to the aid of the priests of the Quebec seminary, and Sulpicians, such as MM. de Queylus, d'Urfé, Dallet and Brehan de Gallinée, arrived at Montreal; MM. François de Salignac-Fénelon and Claude Trouvé had already landed the year before. "I have during the last month," wrote the prelate, "commissioned two most good and virtuous apostles to go to an Iroquois community which has been for some years established quite near us on the northern side of the great Lake Ontario. One is M. de Fénelon, whose name is well-known in Paris, and the other M. Trouvé. We have not yet been able to learn the result of their mission, but we have every reason to hope for its complete success."

While he was enjoining upon these two missionaries, on their departure for the mission on which he was sending them, that they should always remain in good relations with the Jesuit Fathers, he gave them some advice worthy of the most eminent doctors of the Church:—

"A knowledge of the language," he says, "is necessary in order to influence the savages. It is, nevertheless, one of the smallest parts of the equipment of a good missionary, just as in France to speak French well is not what makes a successful preacher. The talents which make good missionaries are:

"1. To be filled with the spirit of God; this spirit must animate our words and our hearts: *Ex abundantia cordis os loquitur.*

"2. To have great prudence in the choice and arrangement of the things which are necessary either to enlighten the understanding or to bend the will; all that does not tend in this direction is labour lost.

"3. To be very assiduous, in order not to lose opportunities of procuring the salvation of souls, and supplying the neglect which is often manifest in neophytes; for, since the devil on his part *circuit tanquam leo rugiens, quærens quem devoret,* so we must be vigilant against his efforts, with care, gentleness and love.

"4. To have nothing in our life and in our manners which may appear to belie what we say, or which may estrange the minds and hearts of those whom we wish to win to God.

"5. We must make ourselves beloved by our gentleness, patience and charity, and win men's minds and hearts to incline them to God. Often a bitter word, an impatient act or a frowning countenance destroys in a moment what has taken a long time to produce.

"6. The spirit of God demands a peaceful and pious heart, not a restless and dissipated one; one should have a joyous and modest countenance; one should avoid jesting and immoderate laughter, and in general all that is contrary to a holy and joyful modesty: *Modestia vestra nota sit omnibus hominibus.*"

The new Sulpicians had been most favourably received by Mgr. de Laval, and the more so since almost all of them belonged to great families and had renounced, like himself, ease and honour, to devote themselves to the rude apostleship of the Canadian missions.

The difficulties between the bishop and the Abbé de Queylus had disappeared, and had left no trace of bitterness in the souls of these two servants of God. M. de Queylus gave good proof of this subsequently; he gave six thousand francs to the hospital of Quebec, of which one thousand were to endow facilities for the treatment of the poor, and five thousand for the maintenance of a choir-nun. His generosity, moreover, was proverbial: "I cannot find a man more grateful for the favour that you have done him than

M. de Queylus," wrote the intendant, Talon, to the minister, Colbert. "He is going to arrange his affairs in France, divide with his brothers, and collect his worldly goods to use them in Canada, at least so he has assured me. If he has need of your protection, he is striving to make himself worthy of it, and I know that he is most zealous for the welfare of this colony. I believe that a little show of benevolence on your part would redouble this zeal, of which I have good evidence, for what you desire the most, the education of the native children, which he furthers with all his might."

The abbé found the seminary in conditions very different from those prevailing at the time of his departure. In 1663, the members of the Company of Notre-Dame of Montreal had made over to the Sulpicians the whole Island of Montreal and the seigniory of St. Sulpice. Their purpose was to assure the future of the three works which they had not ceased, since the birth of their association, to seek to establish: a seminary for the education of priests in the colony, an institution of education for young girls, and a hospital for the care of the sick.

To learn the happy results due to the eloquence of MM. Trouvé and de Fénelon engaged in the evangelization of the tribes encamped to the north of Lake Ontario, or to that of MM. Dollier de Casson and Gallinée preaching on the shores of Lake Erie, one must read the memoirs of the Jesuit Fathers. We must bear in mind that many facts, which might appear to redound too much to the glory of the missionaries, the modesty of these men refused to give to the public. We shall give an example. One day when M. de Fénelon had come down to Quebec, in the summer of 1669, to give account of his efforts to his bishop, Mgr. de Laval begged the missionary to write a short abstract of his labours for the memoirs. "Monseigneur," replied humbly the modest Sulpician, "the greatest favour that you can do us is not to allow us to be mentioned." Will he, at least, like the traveller who, exhausted by fatigue and privation, reaches finally the promised land, repose in Capuan delights? Mother Mary of the Incarnation informs us on this point: "M. l'abbé de Fénelon," says she, "having wintered with the Iroquois, has paid us a visit. I asked him how he had been able to subsist, having had only sagamite[5] as sole provision, and pure water to drink. He replied that he was so accustomed to it that he made no distinction between this food and any other, and that he was about to set out on his return to pass the winter again there with M. de Trouvé, having left him only to go and get the wherewithal to pay the Indians who feed them. The zeal of these great servants of God is admirable."

The activity and the devotion of the Jesuits and of the Sulpicians might thus make up for lack of numbers, and Mgr. de Laval judged that they were amply sufficient for the task of the holy ministry. But the intendant, Talon, feared lest the Society of Jesus should become omnipotent in the colony; adopting from policy the famous device of Catherine de Medici, *divide to rule*, he hoped that an order of mendicant friars would counterbalance the influence of the sons of Loyola, and he brought with him from France, in 1670, Father Allard, Superior of the Récollets in the Province of St. Denis, and four other brothers of the same order. We must confess that, if a new order of monks was to be established in Canada, it was preferable in all justice to apply to that of St. Francis rather than to any others, for had it not traced the first evangelical furrows in the new field and left glorious memories in the colony?

Mgr. de Laval received from the king in 1671 the following letter:

"My Lord Bishop of Petræa:

"Having considered that the re-establishment of the monks of the Order of St. Francis on the lands which they formerly possessed in Canada might be of great avail for the spiritual consolation of my subjects and for the relief of your ecclesiastics in the said country, I send you this letter to tell you that my intention is that you should give to the Rev. Father Allard, the superior, and to the four monks whom he brings with him, the power of administering the sacraments to all those who may have need of them and who may have recourse to these reverend Fathers, and that, moreover, you should aid them with your authority in order that they may resume possession of all which belongs to them in the said country, to all of which I am persuaded you will willingly subscribe, by reason of the knowledge which you have of the relief which my subjects will receive...."

The prelate had not been consulted; moreover, the intervention of the newcomers did not seem to him opportune. But he was obstinate and unapproachable only when he believed his conscience involved; he received the Récollets with great benevolence and rendered them all the service possible. "He gave them abundant aid," says Latour, "and furnished them for more than a year with food and lodging. Although the Order had come in spite of him, he gave them at the outset four missions: Three Rivers, Ile Percé, St.

John's River and Fort Frontenac. These good Fathers were surprised; they did not cease to praise the charity of the bishop, and confessed frankly that, having only come to oppose his clergy, they could not understand why they were so kindly treated."

After all, the breadth of character of these brave heroes of evangelic poverty could not but please the Canadian people; ever gay and pleasant, and of even temper, they traversed the country to beg a meagre pittance. Everywhere received with joy, they were given a place at the common table; they were looked upon as friends, and the people related to them their joys and afflictions. Hardly was a robe of drugget descried upon the horizon when the children rushed forward, surrounded the good Father, and led him by the hand to the family fireside. The Récollets had always a good word for this one, a consolatory speech for that one, and on occasion, brought up as they had been, for the most part under a modest thatched roof, knew how to lend a hand at the plough, or suggest a good counsel if the flock were attacked by somesickness. On their departure, the benediction having been given to all, there was a vigorous handshaking, and already their hosts were discounting the pleasure of a future visit.

On their arrival the Récollet Fathers lodged not far from the Ursuline Convent, till the moment when, their former monastery on the St. Charles River being repaired, they were able to install themselves there. Some years later they built a simple refuge on land granted them in the Upper Town. Finally, having become almoners of the Château St. Louis, where the governor resided, they built their monastery opposite the castle, back to back with the magnificent church which bore the name of St. Anthony of Padua. They reconquered the popularity which they had enjoyed in the early days of the colony, and the bishop entrusted to their devotion numerous parishes and four missions. Unfortunately, they allowed themselves to be so influenced by M. de Frontenac, in spite of repeated warnings from Mgr. de Laval, that they espoused the cause of the governor in the disputes between the latter and the intendant, Duchesneau. Their gratitude towards M. de Frontenac, who always protected them, is easily explained, but it is no less true that they should have respected above all the authority of the prelate who alone had to answer before God for the religious administration of his diocese.

[4] Racine's *Athalie*.

[5] A sort of porridge of water and pounded maize.

CHAPTER VIII

THE PROGRESS OF THE COLONY

This year, 1668, would have brought only consolations to Mgr. de Laval, if, unhappily, M. de Talon had not inflicted a painful blow upon the heart of the prelate: the commissioner obtained from the Sovereign Council a decree permitting the unrestricted sale of intoxicating drinks both to the savages and to the French, and only those who became intoxicated might be sentenced to a slight penalty. This was opening the way for the greatest abuses, and no later than the following year Mother Mary of the Incarnation wrote: "What does the most harm here is the traffic in wine and brandy. We preach against those who give these liquors to the savages; and yet many reconcile their consciences to the permission of this thing. They go into the woods and carry drinks to the savages in order to get their furs for nothing when they are drunk. Immorality, theft and murder ensue.... We had not yet seen the French commit such crimes, and we can attribute the cause of them only to the pernicious traffic in brandy."

Commissioner Talon was, however, the cleverest administrator that the colony had possessed, and the title of the "Canadian Colbert" which Bibaud confers upon him is well deserved. Mother Incarnation summed up his merits well in the following terms: "M. Talon is leaving us," said she, "and returning to France, to the great regret of everybody and to the loss of all Canada, for since he has been here in the capacity of commissioner the country has progressed and its business prospered more than they had done since the French occupation." Talon worked with all his might in developing the resources of the colony, by exploiting the mines, by encouraging the fisheries, agriculture, the exportation of timber, and general commerce, and especially by inducing, through the gift of a few acres of ground, the majority of the soldiers of the regiment of Carignan to remain in the country. He entered every house to enquire of possible complaints; he took the first census, and laid out three villages near Quebec. His plans for the future were vaster still: he recommended the king to buy or conquer the districts of Orange and Manhattan; moreover, according to Abbé Ferland, he dreamed of connecting Canada with the Antilles in commerce. With this purpose he had had a ship built at Quebec, and had bought another in order to begin at once. This very first year he sent to the markets of Martinique and Santo Domingo fresh and dry cod, salted salmon, eels, pease, seal and porpoise oil, clapboards and planks. He had different kinds of wood cut in order to try them, and he exported masts to La Rochelle, which he hoped to see used in the shipyards of the Royal Navy. He proposed to Colbert the establishment of a brewery, in order to utilize the barley and the wheat, which in a few years would be so abundant that the farmer could not sell them. This was, besides, a means of preventing drunkenness, and of retaining in the country the sum of one hundred thousand francs, which went out each year for the purchase of wines and brandies. M. Talon presented at the same time to the minister the observations which he had made on the French population of the country. "The people," said Talon, "are a mosaic, and though composed of colonists from different provinces of France whose temperaments do not always sympathize, they seem to me harmonious enough. There are," he added, "among these colonists people in easy circumstances, indigent people and people between these two extremes."

But he thought only of the material development of the colony; upon others, he thought, were incumbent the responsibility for and defence of spiritual interests. He was mistaken, for, although he had not in his power the direction of souls, his duties as a simple soldier of the army of Christ imposed upon him none the less the obligation of avoiding all that might contribute to the loss of even a single soul. The disorders which were the inevitable result of a free traffic in intoxicating liquors, finally assumed such proportions that the council, without going as far as the absolute prohibition of the sale of brandy to the Indians, restricted, nevertheless, this deplorable traffic; it forbade under the most severe penalties the carrying of firewater into the woods to the savages, but it continued to tolerate the sale of intoxicating liquors in the French settlements. It seems that Cavelier de la Salle himself, in his store at Lachine where he dealt with the Indians, did not scruple to sell them this fatal poison.

From 1668 to 1670, during the two years that Commissioner Talon had to spend in France, both for reasons of health and on account of family business, he did not cease to work actively at the court for his beloved Canada. M. de Bouteroue, who took his place during his absence, managed to prejudice the minds of the colonists in his favour by his exquisite urbanity and the polish of his manners.

It will not be out of place, we think, to give here some details of the state of the country and its resources at this period. Since the first companies in charge of Canada were formed principally of merchants of Rouen, of La Rochelle and of St. Malo, it is not astonishing that the first colonists should have come largely from Normandy and Perche. It was only about 1660 that fine and vigorous offspring increased a population which up to that time was renewed only through immigration; in the early days, in fact, the colonists lost all their children, but they found in this only a new reason for hope in the future. "Since God takes the first fruits," said they, "He will save us the rest." The wise and far-seeing mind of Cardinal Richelieu had understood that agricultural development was the first condition of success for a young colony, and his efforts in this direction had been admirably seconded both by Commissioner Talon and Mgr. de Laval at Quebec, and by the Company of Montreal, which had not hesitated at any sacrifice in order to establish at Ville-Marie a healthy and industrious population. If the reader doubts this, let him read the letters of Talon, of Mother Mary of the Incarnation, of Fathers Le Clercq and Charlevoix, of M. Aubert and many others. "Great care had been exercised," says Charlevoix, "in the selection of candidates who had presented themselves for the colonization of New France.... As to the girls who were sent out to be married to the new inhabitants, care was always taken to enquire of their conduct before they embarked, and their subsequent behaviour was a proof of the success of this system. During the following years the same care was exercised, and we soon saw in this part of America a generation of true Christians growing up, among whom prevailed the simplicity of the first centuries of the Church, and whose posterity has not yet lost sight of the great examples set by their ancestors.... In justice to the colony of New France we must admit that the source of almost all the families which still survive there to-day is pure and free from those stains which opulence can hardly efface; this is because the first settlers were either artisans always occupied in useful labour, or persons of good family who came there with the sole intention of living there more tranquilly and preserving their religion in greater security. I fear the less contradiction upon this head since I have lived with some of these first colonists, all people still more respectable by reason of their honesty, their frankness and the firm piety which they profess than by their white hair and the memory of the services which they rendered to the colony."

M. Aubert says, on his part: "The French of Canada are well built, nimble and vigorous, enjoying perfect health, capable of enduring all sorts of fatigue, and warlike; which is the reason why, during the last war, French-Canadians received a fourth more pay than the French of Europe. All these advantageous physical qualities of the French-Canadians arise from the fact that they have been born in a good climate, and nourished by good and abundant food, that they are at liberty to engage from childhood in fishing, hunting, and journeying in canoes, in which there is much exercise. As to bravery, even if it were not born with them as Frenchmen, the manner of warfare of the Iroquois and other savages of this continent, who burn alive almost all their prisoners with incredible cruelty, caused the French to face ordinary death in battle as a boon rather than be taken alive; so that they fight desperately and with great indifference to life." The consequence of this judicious method of peopling a colony was that, the trunk of the tree being healthy and vigorous, the branches were so likewise.

"It was astonishing," wrote Mother Mary of the Incarnation, "to see the great number of beautiful and well-made children, without any corporeal deformity unless through accident. A poor man will have eight or more children, who in the winter go barefooted and bareheaded, with a little shirt upon their back, and who live only on eels and bread, and nevertheless are plump and large."

Property was feudal, as in France, and this constitution was maintained even after the conquest of the country by the English. Vast stretches of land were granted to those who seemed, thanks to their state of fortune, fit to form centres of population, and these seigneurs granted in their turn parts of these lands to the immigrants for a rent of from one to three cents per acre, according to the value of the land, besides a tribute in grain and poultry. The indirect taxation consisted of the obligation of maintaining the necessary roads, one day's compulsory labour per year, convertible into a payment of forty cents, the right of *mouture*, consisting of a pound of flour on every fourteen from the common mill, finally the payment of a twelfth in case of transfer and sale (stamp and registration). This seigniorial tenure was burdensome, we must admit, though it was less crushing than that which weighed upon husbandry in France before the Revolution. The farmers of Canada uttered a long sigh of relief when it was abolished by the legislature in 1867.

The habits of this population were remarkably simple; the costume of some of our present out-of-door clubs gives an accurate idea of the dress of that time, which was the same for all: the garment of wool, the cloak, the belt of arrow pattern, and the woollen cap, called tuque, formed the national costume. And not only did the colonists dress without the slightest affectation, but they even made their clothes themselves. "The growing of hemp," says the Abbé Ferland, "was encouraged, and succeeded wonderfully. They used the nettle to make strong cloths; looms set up in each house in the village furnished drugget, bolting cloth, serge and ordinary cloth. The leathers of the country sufficed for a great portion of the needs of the population. Accordingly, after enumerating the advances in agriculture and industry, Talon announced to Colbert with just satisfaction, that he could clothe himself from head to foot in Canadian products, and that in a short time the colony, if it were well administered, would draw from Old France only a few objects of prime need."

The interior of the dwellings was not less simple, and we find still in our country districts a goodly number of these old French houses; they had only one single room, in which the whole family ate, lived and slept, and received the light through three windows. At the back of the room was the bed of the parents, supported by the wall, in another corner a couch, used as a seat during the day and as a bed for the children during the night, for the top was lifted off as one lifts the cover of a box. Built into the wall, generally at the right of the entrance, was the stone chimney, whose top projected a little above the roof; the stewpan, in which the food was cooked, was hung in the fireplace from a hook. Near the hearth a staircase, or rather a ladder, led to the loft, which was lighted by two windows cut in the sides, and which held the grain. Finally a table, a few chairs or benches completed these primitive furnishings, though we must not forget to mention the old gun hung above the bed to be within reach of the hand in case of a night surprise from the dreaded Iroquois.

In peaceful times, too, the musket had its service, for at this period every Canadian was born a disciple of St. Hubert. We must confess that this great saint did not refuse his protection in this country, where, with a single shot, a hunter killed, in 1663, a hundred and thirty wild pigeons. These birds were so tame that one might kill them with an oar on the bank of the river, and so numerous that the colonists, after having gathered and salted enough for their winter's provision, abandoned the rest to the dogs and pigs. How many hunters of our day would have displayed their skill in these fortunate times! This abundance of pigeons at a period when our ancestors were not favoured in the matter of food as we are to-day, recalls at once to our memory the quail that Providence sent to the Jews in the desert; and it is a fact worthy of mention that as soon as our forefathers could dispense with this superabundance of game, the wild pigeons disappeared so totally and suddenly that the most experienced hunters cannot explain this sudden disappearance. There were found also about Ville-Marie many partridge and duck, and since the colonists could not go out after game in the woods, where they would have been exposed to the ambuscades of the Iroquois, the friendly Indians brought to market the bear, the elk, the deer, the buffalo, the caribou, the beaver and the muskrat. On fast days the Canadians did not lack for fish; eels were sold at five francs a hundred, and in June, 1649, more than three hundred sturgeons were caught at Montreal within a fortnight. The shad, the pike, the wall-eyed pike, the carp, the brill, the maskinonge were plentiful, and there was besides, more particularly at Quebec, good herring and salmon fishing, while at Malbaie (Murray Bay) codfish, and at Three Rivers white fish were abundant.

At first, food, clothing and property were all paid for by exchange of goods. Men bartered, for example, a lot of ground for two cows and a pair of stockings; a more considerable piece of land was to be had for two oxen, a cow and a little money. "Poverty," says Bossuet, speaking of other nations, "was not an evil; on the contrary, they looked upon it as a means of keeping their liberty more intact, there being nothing freer or more independent than a man who knows how to live on little, and who, without expecting anything from the protection or the largess of others, relies for his livelihood only on his industry and labour." Voltaire has said with equal justice: "It is not the scarcity of money, but that of men and talent, which makes an empire weak."

On the arrival of the royal troops coin became less rare. "Money is now common," wrote Mother Incarnation, "these gentlemen having brought much of it. They pay cash for all they buy, both food and other necessaries." Money was worth a fourth more than in France, thus fifteen cents were worth twenty. As a natural consequence, two currencies were established in New France, and the *livre tournois* (French franc) was distinguished from the franc of the country. The Indians were dealt with by exchanges, and one might see them traversing the streets of Quebec, Montreal or Three Rivers, offering from house to house rich furs, which they bartered for blankets, powder, lead, but above all, for that accursed firewater which caused such havoc among them, and such interminable disputes between the civil and the religious power. Intoxicating liquors were the source of many disorders, and we cannot too much regret that this stain rested upon the glory of New France. Yet such a society, situated in what was undeniably a difficult position, could not be expected to escape every imperfection.

The activity and the intelligence of Mgr. de Laval made themselves felt in every beneficent and progressive work. He could not remain indifferent to the education of his flock; we find him as zealous for the progress of primary education as for the development of his two seminaries or his school at St. Joachim. Primary instruction was given first by the good Récollets at Quebec, at Tadousac and at Three Rivers. The Jesuits replaced them, and were able, thanks to the munificence of the son of the Marquis de Gamache, to add a college to their elementary school at Quebec. At Ville-Marie the Sulpicians, with never-failing abnegation, not content with the toil of their ministry, lent themselves to the arduous task of teaching; the venerable superior himself, M. Souart, took the modest title of headmaster. From a healthy bud issues a fine fruit: just as the smaller seminary of Quebec gave birth to the Laval University, so from the school of M. Souart sprang in 1733 the College of Montreal, transferred forty years later to the Château Vaudreuil, on Jacques Cartier Square; then to College Street, now St. Paul Street. The college rises to-day on an admirable site on the slope of the mountain; the main seminary, which adjoins it, seems to dominate the city stretched at its feet, as the two sister sciences taught there, theology and philosophy, dominate by their importance the other branches of human knowledge.

M. de Fénelon, who was already devoted to the conversion of the savages in the famous mission of Montreal mountain, gave the rest of his time to the training of the young Iroquois; he gathered them in a school erected by his efforts near Pointe Claire, on the Dorval Islands, which he had received from M. de Frontenac. Later on the Brothers Charron established a house at Montreal with a double purpose of charity: to care for the poor and the sick, and to train men in order to send them to open schools in the country district. This institution, in spite of the enthusiasm of its founders, did not succeed, and became extinct about the middle of the eighteenth century. Finally, in 1838, Canada greeted with joy the arrival of the sons of the blessed Jean Baptiste de la Salle, the Brothers of the Christian Doctrine, so well known throughout the world for their modesty and success in teaching.

The girls of the colony were no less well looked after than the boys; at Quebec, the Ursuline nuns, established in that city by Madame de la Peltrie, trained them for the future irreproachable mothers of families. The attempts made to Gallicize the young savages met with no success in the case of the boys, but were better rewarded by the young Indian girls. "We have Gallicized," writes Mother Mary of the Incarnation, "a number of Indian girls, both Hurons and Algonquins, whom we subsequently married to Frenchmen, who get along with them very well. There is one among them who reads and writes to perfection, both in her native Huron tongue and in French; no one can discern or believe that she was born a savage. The commissioner was so delighted at this that he induced her to write for him something in the two languages, in order to take it to France and show it as an extraordinary production." Further on she adds, "It is a very difficult thing, not to say impossible, to Gallicize or civilize them. We have more experience in this than any one else, and we have observed that of a hundred who have passed through our hands we have hardly civilized one. We find in them docility and intelligence, but when we least expect it, they climb over our fence and go off to run the woods with their parents, where they find more pleasure than in all the comforts of our French houses."

At Montreal it was the venerable Marguerite Bourgeoys who began to teach in a poor hovel the rudiments of the French tongue. This humble school was transformed a little more than two centuries later into one of the most vast and imposing edifices of the city of Montreal. Fire destroyed it in 1893, but we must hope that this majestic monument of Ville-Marie will soon rise again from its ruins to become the centre of operations of the numerous educational institutions of the Congregation of Notre-Dame which cover our country. M. l'abbé Verreau, the much regretted principal of the Jacques Cartier Normal School, appreciates in these terms the services rendered to education by Mother Bourgeoys, a woman eminent from all points of view: "The Congregation of Notre-Dame," says he, "is a truly national institution, whose ramifications extend beyond the limits of Canada. Marguerite Bourgeoys took in hand the education of the women of the people, the basis of society. She taught young women to become what they ought to be, especially at this period, women full of moral force, of modesty, of courage in the face of the dangers in the midst of which they lived. If the French-Canadians have preserved a certain character of politeness and urbanity, which strangers are not slow in admitting, they owe it in a great measure to the work of Marguerite Bourgeoys."

CHAPTER IX

BECOMES BISHOP OF QUEBEC

The creation of a bishopric in Canada was becoming necessary, and all was ready for the erection of a separate see. Mgr. de Laval had thought of everything: the two seminaries with the resources indispensable for their maintenance, cathedral, parishes or missions regularly established, institutions of education or charity, numerous schools, a zealous and devoted clergy, respected both by the government of the colony and by that of the mother country. What more could be desired? He had many struggles to endure in order to obtain this creation, but patience and perseverance never failed him, and like the drop of water which, falling incessantly upon the pavement, finally wears away the stone, his reasonable and ever repeated demands eventually overcame the obstinacy of the king. Not, however, until 1674 was he definitely appointed Bishop of Quebec, and could enjoy without opposition a title which had belonged to him so long in reality; this was, as it were, the final consecration of his life and the crowning of his efforts. Upon the news of this the joy of the people and of the clergy rose to its height: the future of the Canadian Church was assured, and she would inscribe in her annals a name dear to all and soon to be glorified.

Shall we, then, suppose that this pontiff was indeed ambitious, who, coming in early youth to wield his pastoral crozier upon the banks of the St. Lawrence, did not fear the responsibility of so lofty a task? The assumption would be quite unjustified. Rather let us think of him as meditating on this text of St. Paul: "*Oportet episcopum irreprehensibilem esse,"* the bishop must be irreproachable in his house, his relations, his speech and even his silence. His past career guaranteed his possession of that admixture of strength and gentleness, of authority and condescension in which lies the great art of governing men. Moreover, one thing reassured him, his knowledge that the crown of a bishop is often a crown of thorns. When the apostle St. Paul outlined for his disciple the main features of the episcopal character, he spoke not alone for the immediate successors of the apostles, but for all those who in the succession of ages should be honoured by the same dignity. No doubt the difficulties would be often less, persecution might even cease entirely, but trial would continue always, because it is the condition of the Church as well as that of individuals. The prelate himself explains to us the very serious reasons which led him to insist on obtaining the title of Bishop of Quebec. He writes in these terms to the Propaganda: "I have never till now sought the episcopacy, and I have accepted it in spite of myself, convinced of my weakness. But, having borne its burden, I shall consider it a boon to be relieved of it, though I do not refuse to sacrifice myself for the Church of Jesus Christ and for the welfare of souls. I have, however, learned by long experience how unguarded is the position of an apostolic vicar against those who are entrusted with political affairs, I mean the officers of the court, perpetual rivals and despisers of the ecclesiastical power, who have nothing more common to object than that the authority of the apostolic vicar is doubtful and should be restricted within certain limits. This is why, after having maturely considered everything, I have resolved to resign this function and to return no more to New France unless a see be erected there, and unless I be provided and furnished with bulls constituting me its occupant. Such is the purpose of my journey to France and the object of my desires."

As early as the year 1662, at the time of his first journey to France, the Bishop of Petræa had obtained from Louis XIV the assurance that this prince would petition the sovereign pontiff for the erection of the see of Quebec; moreover, the monarch had at the same time assigned to the future bishopric the revenues of the abbey of Maubec. The king kept his word, for on June 28th, 1664, he addressed to the common Father of the faithful the following letter: "The choice made by your Holiness of the person of the Sieur de Laval, Bishop of Petræa, to go in the capacity of apostolic vicar to exercise episcopal functions in Canada has been attended by many advantages to this growing Church. We have reason to expect still greater results if it please your Holiness to permit him to continue there the same functions in the capacity of bishop of the place, by establishing for this purpose an episcopal see in Quebec; and we hope that your Holiness will be the more inclined to this since we have already provided for the maintenance of the bishop and his canons by consenting to the perpetual union of the abbey of Maubec with the future bishopric. This is why we beg you to grant to the Bishop of Petræa the title of Bishop of Quebec upon our nomination and prayer, with power to exercise in this capacity the episcopal functions in all Canada."

However, the appointment was not consummated; the Propaganda, indeed, decided in a rescript of December 15th, 1666, that it was necessary to make of Quebec a see, whose occupant should be appointed by the king; the Consistorial Congregation of Rome promulgated a new decree with the same purpose on October 9th,

1670, and yet Mgr. de Laval still remained Bishop of Petræa. This was because the eternal question of jurisdiction as between the civil and religious powers, the question which did so much harm to Catholicism in France, in England, in Italy, and especially in Germany, was again being revived. The King of France demanded that the new diocese should be dependent upon the Metropolitan of Rouen, while the pontifical government, of which its providential rôle requires always a breadth of view, and, so to speak, a foreknowledge of events impossible to any nation, desired the new diocese to be an immediate dependency of the Holy See. "We must confess here," says the Abbé Ferland, "that the sight of the sovereign pontiff reached much farther into the future than that of the great king. Louis XIV was concerned with the kingdom of France; Clement X thought of the interests of the whole Catholic world. The little French colony was growing; separated from the mother country by the ocean, it might be wrested from France by England, which was already so powerful in America; what, then, would become of the Church of Quebec if it had been wont to lean upon that of Rouen and to depend upon it? It was better to establish at once immediate relations between the Bishop of Quebec and the supreme head of the Catholic Church; it was better to establish bonds which could be broken neither by time nor force, and Quebec might thus become one day the metropolis of the dioceses which should spring from its bosom."

The opposition to the views of Mgr. de Laval did not come, however, so much from the king as from Mgr. de Harlay, Archbishop of Rouen, who had never consented to the detachment of Canada from his jurisdiction. Events turned out fortunately for the apostolic vicar, since the Archbishop of Rouen was called to the important see of Paris on the death of the Archbishop of Paris, Hardouin de Péréfixe de Beaumont, in the very year in which Mgr. de Laval embarked for France, accompanied by his grand vicar, M. de Lauson-Charny. The task now became much easier, and Laval had no difficulty in inducing the king to urge the erection of the diocese at Quebec, and to abandon his claims to making the new diocese dependent on the archbishopric of Rouen.

Before leaving Canada the Bishop of Quebec had entrusted the administration of the apostolic vicariate to M. de Bernières, and, in case of the latter's death, to M. Dudouyt. He embarked in the autumn of 1671.

To the keen regret of the population of Ville-Marie, which owed him so much, M. de Queylus, Abbé de Loc-Dieu and superior of the Seminary of Montreal for the last three years, went to France at the same time as his ecclesiastical superior. "M. l'abbé de Queylus," wrote Commissioner Talon to the Minister Colbert, "is making an urgent application for the settlement and increase of the colony of Montreal. He carries his zeal farther, for he is going to take charge of the Indian children who fall into the hands of the Iroquois, in order to have them educated, the boys in his seminary, and the girls by persons of the same sex, who form at Montreal a sort of congregation to teach young girls the petty handicrafts, in addition to reading and writing." M. de Queylus had used his great fortune in all sorts of good works in the colony, but he was not the only Sulpician whose hand was always ready and willing. Before dying, M. Olier had begged his successors to continue the work at Ville-Marie, "because," said he, "it is the will of

God," and the priests of St. Sulpice received this injunction as one of the most sacred codicils of the will of their Father. However onerous the continuation of this plan was for the company, the latter sacrificed to it without hesitation its resources, its efforts and its members with the most complete abnegation.[6] Thus when, on March 9th, 1663, the Company of Montreal believed itself no longer capable of meeting its obligations, and begged St. Sulpice to take them up, the seminary subordinated all considerations of self-interest and human prudence to this view. To this MM. de Bretonvilliers, de Queylus and du Bois devoted their fortunes, and to this work of the conversion of the savages priests distinguished in birth and riches gave up their whole lives and property. M. de Belmont discharged the hundred and twenty thousand francs of debts of the Company of Montreal, gave as much more to the establishment of divers works, and left more than two hundred thousand francs of his patrimony to support them after his death. How many others did likewise! During more than fifty years Paris sent to this mission only priests able to pay their board, that they might have the right to share in this evangelization. This disinterestedness, unheard of in the history of the most unselfish congregations, saved, sustained and finally developed this settlement, to which Roman Catholics point to-day with pride. The Seminary of Paris contributed to it a sum equal to twice the value of the island, and during the first sixty years more than nine hundred thousand francs, as one may see by the archives of the Department of Marine at Paris. These sums to-day would represent a large fortune.

Finally the prayers of Mgr. de Laval were heard; Pope Clement X signed on October 1st, 1674, the bulls establishing the diocese of Quebec, which was to extend over all the French possessions in North America. The sovereign pontiff incorporated with the new bishopric for its maintenance the abbey of Maubec, given by the King of France already in 1662, and in exchange for the renunciation by this prince of his right of presentation to the abbey of Maubec, granted him the right of nomination to the bishopric of Quebec. To his first gift the king had added a second, that of the abbey of Lestrées. Situated in Normandy and in the archdeaconry of Evreux, this abbey was one of the oldest of the order of Cîteaux.

Up to this time the venerable bishop had had many difficulties to surmount; he was about to meet some of another sort, those of the administration of vast properties. The abbey of Maubec, occupied by monks of the order of St. Benedict, was situated in one of the fairest provinces of France, Le Perry, and was dependent upon the archdiocese of Bourges. Famous vineyards, verdant meadows, well cultivated fields, rich farms, forests full of game and ponds full of fish made this abbey an admirable domain; unfortunately, the expenses of maintaining or repairing the buildings, the dues payable to the government, the allowances secured to the monks, and above all, the waste and theft which must necessarily victimize proprietors separated from their tenants by the whole breadth of an ocean, must absorb a great part of the revenues. Letters of the steward of this property to the Bishop of Quebec are instructive in this matter. "M. Porcheron is still the same," writes the steward, M. Matberon, "and bears me a grudge because I desire to safeguard your interests. I am incessantly carrying on the work of needful repairs in all the places dependent on Maubec, chiefly those necessary to the ponds, in order that M. Porcheron may have no damages against you. This is much against his will, for he is constantly seeking an excuse for litigation. He swears that he does not want your farm any longer, but as for me, I believe that this is not his feeling, and that he would wish the farm out of the question, for he is too fond of hunting and his pleasure to quit it.... He does his utmost to remove me from your service, insinuating many things against me which are not true; but this does not lessen my zeal in serving you."

Mgr. de Laval, who did not hesitate at any exertion when it was a question of the interests of his Church, did not fail to go and visit his two abbeys. He set out, happy in the prospect of being able to admire these magnificent properties whose rich revenues would permit him to do so much good in his diocese; but he was painfully affected at the sight of the buildings in ruins, sad relics of the wars of religion. In order to free himself as much as possible from cares which would have encroached too much upon his precious time and his pastoral duties, Laval caused a manager to be appointed by the Royal Council for the abbey of Lestrées, and rented it for a fixed sum to M. Berthelot. He also made with the latter a very advantageous transaction by exchanging with him the Island of Orleans for the Ile Jésus; M. Berthelot was to give him besides a sum of twenty-five thousand francs, which was employed in building the seminary. Later the king made the Island of Orleans a county. It became the county of St. Lawrence.

Mgr. de Laval was too well endowed with qualities of the heart, as well as with those of the mind, not to have preserved a deep affection for his family; he did not fail to go and see them twice during his stay in France. Unhappily, his brother, Jean-Louis, to whom he had yielded all his rights as eldest son, and his titles to the hereditary lordship of Montigny and Montbeaudry, caused only grief to his family and to his wife, Françoise de Chevestre. As lavish as he was violent and hot-tempered, he reduced by his excesses his numerous family (for he had had ten children), to such poverty that the Bishop of Quebec had to come to his aid; besides the assistance which he sent them, the prelate bought him a house. He extended his protection also to his nephews, and his brother, Henri de Laval, wrote to him about them as follows: "The eldest is developing a little; he is in the army with the king, and his father has given him a good start. I have obtained from my petitions from Paris a place as monk in the Congregation of the Cross for his second son, whom I shall try to have reared in the knowledge and fear of God. I believe that the youngest, who has been sent to you, will have come to the right place; he is of good promise. My brother desires greatly that you may have the goodness to give Fanchon the advantage of an education before sending him back. It is a great charity to these poor children to give them a little training. You will be a father to them in this matter." One never applied in vain to the heart of the good bishop. Two of his nephews owed him their education at the seminary of Quebec; one of them, Fanchon (Charles-François-Guy), after a brilliant course in theology at Paris, became vicar-general to the Swan of Cambrai, the illustrious Fénelon, and was later raised to the bishopric of Ypres.

Meanwhile, four years had elapsed since Mgr. de Laval had left the soil of Canada, and he did not cease to receive letters which begged him respectfully to return to his diocese. "Nothing is lacking to animate us but the presence of our lord bishop," wrote, one day, Father Dablon. "His absence keeps this country, as it were, in mourning, and makes us languish in the too long separation from a person so necessary to these growing churches. He was the soul of them, and the zeal which he showed on every occasion for the welfare of our Indians drew upon us favours of Heaven most powerful for the success of our missions; and since, however distant he be in the body, his heart is ever with us, we experience the effects of it in the continuity of the blessings with which God favours the labours of our missionaries." Accordingly, he did not lose a moment after receiving the decrees appointing him Bishop of Quebec. On May 19th, 1675, he renewed the union of his seminary with that of the Foreign Missions in Paris. "This union," says the Abbé Ferland, "a union which he had effected for the first time in 1665 as apostolic bishop of New France, was of great importance to his diocese. He found, indeed, in this institution, good recruits, who were sent to him when needed, and faithful correspondents, whom he could address with confidence, and who had sufficient influence at court to gain a hearing for their representations in favour of the Church in Canada." On May 29th of the same year he set sail for Canada; he was accompanied by a priest, a native of the city of Orleans, M. Glandelet, who was one of the most distinguished priests of the seminary.

To understand with what joy he was received by his parishioners on his arrival, it is enough to read what his brother, Henri de

Laval, wrote to him the following year: "I cannot express to you the satisfaction and inward joy which I have received in my soul on reading a report sent from Canada of the manner in which your clergy and all your people have received you, and that our Lord inspires them all with just and true sentiments to recognize you as their father and pastor. They testify to having received through your beloved person as it were a new life. I ask our Lord every day at His holy altars to preserve you some years more for the sanctification of these poor people and our own."

[6] *Vie de M. Olier*, par De Lanjuère. As I wrote this life some years ago with the collaboration of a gentleman whom death has taken from us, I believe myself entitled to reproduce here and there in the present life of Mgr. de Laval extracts from this book.

CHAPTER X

FRONTENAC IS APPOINTED GOVERNOR

During the early days of the absence of its first pastor, the Church of Canada had enjoyed only days of prosperity; skilfully directed by MM. de Bernières and de Dudouyt, who scrupulously followed the line of conduct laid down for them by Mgr. de Laval before his departure, it was pursuing its destiny peacefully. But this calm, forerunner of the storm, could not last; it was the destiny of the Church, as it had been the lot of nations, to be tossed incessantly by the violent winds of trial and persecution. The difficulties which arose soon reached the acute stage, and all the firmness and tact of the Bishop of Quebec were needed to meet them. The departure of Laval for France in the autumn of 1671 had been closely followed by that of Governor de Courcelles and that of Commissioner Talon. The latter was not replaced until three years later, so that the new governor, Count de Frontenac, who arrived in the autumn of 1672, had no one at his side in the Sovereign Council to oppose his views. This was allowing too free play to the natural despotism of his character. Louis de Buade, Count de Palluau and de Frontenac, lieutenant-general of the king'sarmies, had previously served in Holland under the illustrious Maurice, Prince of Orange, then in France, Italy and Germany, and his merit had gained for him the reputation of a great captain. The illustrious Turenne entrusted to him the command of the reinforcements sent to Candia when that island was besieged by the Turks. He had a keen mind, trained by serious study; haughty towards the powerful of this world, he was affable to ordinary people, and thus made for himself numerous enemies, while remaining very popular. Father Charlevoix has drawn an excellent portrait of him: "His heart was greater than his birth, his wit lively, penetrating, sound, fertile and highly cultivated: but he was biased by the most unjust prejudices, and capable of carrying them very far. He wished to rule alone, and there was nothing he would not do to remove those whom he was afraid of finding in his way. His worth and ability were equal; no one knew better how to assume over the people whom he governed and with whom he had to deal, that ascendency so necessary to keep them in the paths of duty and respect. He won when he wished it the friendship of the French and their allies, and never has general treated his enemies with more dignity and nobility. His views for the aggrandizement of the colony were large and true, but his prejudices sometimes prevented the execution of plans which depended on him.... He justified, in one of the most critical circumstances of his life, the opinion that his ambition and the desire of preserving his authority had more power over him than his zeal for the public good. The fact is that there is no virtue which does not belie itself when one has allowed a dominant passion to gain the upper hand. The Count de Frontenac might have been a great prince if Heaven had placed him on the throne, but he had dangerous faults for a subject who is not well persuaded that his glory consists in sacrificing everything to the service of his sovereign and the public utility."

It was under the administration of Frontenac that the Compagnie des Indes Occidentales, which had accepted in 1663 a portion of the obligations and privileges of the Company of the Cent-Associés, renounced its rights over New France. Immediately after his arrival he began the construction of Fort Cataraqui; if we are to believe some historians, motives of personal interest guided him in the execution of this enterprise; he thought only, it seems, of founding considerable posts for the fur trade, favouring those traders who would consent to give him a share in their profits. The work was urged on with energy. La Salle obtained from the king, thanks to the support of Frontenac, letters patent of nobility, together with the ownership and jurisdiction of the new fort.

With the approval of the governor, Commissioner Talon's plan of having the course of the Mississippi explored was executed by two bold men: Louis Joliet, citizen of Quebec, already known for previous voyages and for his deep knowledge of the Indian tongues, and the devoted missionary, Father Marquette. Without other provisions than Indian corn and dried meat they set out in two bark canoes from Michilimackinac on May 17th, 1673; only five Frenchmen accompanied them. They reached the Mississippi, after having passed the Baie des Puants and the rivers Outagami and Wisconsin, and ascended the stream for more than sixty leagues. They were cordially received by the tribe of the Illinois, which was encamped not far from the river, and Father Marquette promised to return and visit them. The two travellers reached the Arkansas River and learned that the sea was not far distant, but fearing they might fall into the hands of hostile Spaniards, they decided to retrace their steps, and reached the Baie des Puants about the end of September.

The following year Father Marquette wished to keep his promise given to the Illinois. His health is weakened by the trials of a long mission, but what matters this to him? There are souls to save. He preaches the truths of religion to the poor savages gathered in attentive silence; but his strength diminishes, and he regretfully resumes the road to Michilimackinac. He did not have time to reach it, but died near the mouth of a river which long bore his name. His two comrades dug a grave for the remains of the missionary and raised a cross near the tomb. Two years later these sacred bones were transferred with the greatest respect to St. Ignace de Michilimackinac by the savage tribe of the Kiskakons, whom Father Marquette had christianized.

With such an adventurous character as he possessed, Cavelier de la Salle could not learn of the exploration of the course of the Upper Mississippi without burning with the desire to complete the discovery and to descend the river to its mouth. Robert René Cavelier de la Salle was born at Rouen about the year 1644. He belonged to an excellent family, and was well educated. From his earliest years he was passionately fond of stories of travel, and the older he grew the more cramped he felt in the civilization of Europe; like the mettled mustang of the vast prairies of America, he longed for the immensity of unknown plains, for the imposing majesty of forests which the foot of man had not yet trod. Maturity and reason gave a more definite aim to these aspirations; at the age of twenty-four he came to New France to try his fortune. He entered into relations with different Indian tribes, and the extent of his commerce led him to establish a trading-post opposite the Sault St. Louis. This site, as we shall see, received soon after the name of Lachine. Though settled at this spot, La Salle did not cease to meditate on the plan fixed in his brain of discovering a passage to China and the Indies, and upon learning the news that MM. Dollier de Casson and Gallinée were going to christianize the wild tribes of south-western Canada, he hastened to rejoin the two devoted missionaries. They set out in the summer of 1669, with twenty-two Frenchmen. Arriving at Niagara, La Salle suddenly changed his mind, and abandoned his travelling companions, under the pretext of illness. No more was needed for the Frenchman, *né malin*,[7] to fix upon the seigniory of the future discoverer of the mouth of the Mississippi the name of Lachine; M. Dollier de Casson is suspected of being the author of this gentle irony.

Eight years later the explorations of Joliet and Father Marquette revived his instincts as a discoverer; he betook himself to France in 1677 and easily obtained authority to pursue, at his own expense, the discovery already begun. Back in Canada the following year, La Salle thoroughly prepared for this expedition, accumulating provisions at Fort Niagara, and visiting the Indian tribes. In 1679, accompanied by the Chevalier de Tonti, he set out at the head of a small troop, and passed through Michilimackinac, then through the Baie des Puants. From there he reached the Miami River, where he erected a small fort, ascended the Illinois, and, reaching a camp of the Illinois Indians, made an alliance with this tribe, obtaining from them permission to erect upon their soil a fort which he called Crèvecœur. He left M. de Tonti there with a few men and two Récollet missionaries, Fathers de la Ribourde and Membré, and set out again with all haste for Fort Frontenac, for he was very anxious regarding the condition of his own affairs. He had reason to be. "His creditors," says the Abbé Ferland, "had had his goods seized after his departure from Fort Frontenac; his brigantine *Le Griffon* had been lost, with furs valued at thirty thousand francs; his employees had appropriated his goods; a ship which was bringing him from France a cargo valued at twenty-two thousand francs had been wrecked on the Islands of St. Pierre; some canoes laden with merchandise had been dashed to pieces on the journey between Montreal and Frontenac; the men whom he had brought from France had fled to New York, taking a portion of his goods, and already a conspiracy was on foot to disaffect the Canadians in his service. In one word, according to him, the whole of Canada had conspired against his enterprise, and the Count de Frontenac was the only one who consented to support him in the midst of his misfortunes." His remarkable energy and activity remedied this host of evils, and he set out again for Fort Crèvecœur. To cap the climax of his misfortunes, he found it abandoned; being attacked by the Iroquois, whom the English had aroused against them, Tonti and his comrades had been forced to hasty flight. De la Salle found them again at Michilimackinac, but he had the sorrow of learning of the loss of Father de la Ribourde, whom the Illinois had massacred. Tonti and his companions, in their flight, had been obliged to abandon an unsafe canoe, which had carried them half-way, and to continue their journey on foot. Such a series of misfortunes would have discouraged any other than La Salle; on the contrary, he made Tonti and Father Membré retrace their steps. Arriving with them at the Miami fort, he reinforced his little troop by twenty-three Frenchmen and eighteen Indians, and reached Fort Crèvecœur. On February 6th, 1682, he reached the mouth of the Illinois, and then descended the Mississippi. Towards the end of this same month the bold explorers stopped at the juncture of the Ohio with the Father of Rivers, and erected there Fort Prudhomme. On what is Fame dependent? A poor and unknown man, a modest collaborator with La Salle, had the honour of giving his name to this little fort because he had been lost in the neighbourhood and had reached camp nine days later.

Providence was finally about to reward so much bravery and perseverance. The sailor who from the yards of Christopher Columbus's caravel, uttered the triumphant cry of "Land! land!" did not cause more joy to the illustrious Genoese navigator than La Salle received from the sight of the sea so ardently sought. On April 9th La Salle and his comrades could at length admire the immense blue sheet of the Gulf of Mexico. Like Christopher Columbus, who made it his first duty on touching the soil of the New World to fall upon his knees to return thanks to Heaven, La Salle's first business was to raise a cross upon the shore. Father Membré intoned the Te Deum. They then raised the arms of the King of France, in whose name La Salle took possession of the Mississippi, and of all the territories watered by the tributaries of the great river.

Their trials were not over: the risks to be run in traversing so many regions inhabited by barbarians were as great and as numerous after success as before. La Salle was, moreover, delayed for forty days by a serious illness, but God in His goodness did not wish to deprive the valiant discoverers of the fruits of their efforts, and all arrived safe and sound at the place whence they had started. After having passed a year in establishing trading-posts among the Illinois, La Salle appointed M. de Tonti his representative for the time being, and betook himself to France with the intention of giving an account of his journey to the most Christian monarch. His enemies had already forestalled him at the court; we have to seek the real cause of this hatred in the jealousy of traders who feared to find in the future colonists of the western and southern country competitors in their traffic. But far from listening to them, the son of Colbert, Seignelay, then minister of commerce, highly praised the valiant explorer, and sent, in 1684, four ships with two hundred and eighty colonists to people Louisiana, this new gem in the crown of France. But La Salle has not yet finally drained the cup of disappointment, for few men have been so overwhelmed as he by the persistence of ill-fortune. It was not enough that the leader of the expedition should be incapable, the colonists must needs be of a continual evil character, the soldiers undisciplined, the workmen unskilful, the pilot ignorant. They pass the mouth of the Mississippi, near which they should have disembarked, and arrive in Texas; the commander refuses to send the ship about, and La Salle makes up his mind to land where they are. Through the neglect of the pilot, the vessel which was carrying the provisions is cast ashore, then a gale arises which swallows up the tools, the merchandise and the ammunition. The Indians, like birds of prey, hasten up to pillage, and massacre two volunteers. The colonists in exasperation revolt, and stupidly blame La Salle. He saves them, nevertheless, by his energy, and makes them raise a fort with the wreck of the ships. They pass two years there in a famine of everything; twice La Salle tries to find, at the cost of a thousand sufferings, a way of rescue, and twice he fails. Finally, when there remain no more than thirty men, he chooses the ten most resolute, and tries to reach Canada on foot. He did not reach it: on May 20th, 1687, he was murdered by one of his comrades. "Such was the end of this daring adventurer," says Bancroft.[8] "For force of will, and vast conceptions; for various knowledge and quick adaptation of his genius to untried circumstances; for a sublime magnanimity that resigned itself to the will of Heaven and yet triumphed over affliction by energy of purpose and unfaltering hope, he had no superior among his countrymen.... He will be remembered in the great central valley of the West."

It was with deep feelings of joy that Mgr. de Laval, still in France at this period, had read the detailed report of the voyage of discovery made by Joliet and Father Marquette. But the news which he received from Canada was not always so comforting; he felt especially deeply the loss of two great benefactresses of Canada, Madame de la Peltrie and Mother Incarnation. The former had used her entire fortune in founding the Convent of the Ursulines at Quebec. Heaven had lavished its gifts upon her; endowed with brilliant qualities, and adding riches to beauty, she was happy in possessing these advantages only because they allowed her to offer them to the Most High, who had given them to her. She devoted herself to the Christian education of young girls, and passed in Canada the last thirty-two years of her life. The Abbé Casgrain draws the following portrait of her: "Her whole person presented a type of attractiveness and gentleness. Her face, a beautiful oval, was remarkable for the harmony of its lines and the perfection of its contour. A slightly aquiline nose, a clear cut and always smiling mouth, a limpid look veiled by long lashes which the habit of meditation kept half lowered, stamped her features with an exquisite sweetness. Though her frail and delicate figure did not exceed medium height, and though everything about her breathed modesty and humility, her gait was nevertheless full of dignity and nobility; one recognized, in seeing her, the descendant of those great and powerful lords, of those perfect knights whose valiant swords had sustained throne and altar. Through the most charming simplicity there were ever manifest the grand manner of the seventeenth century and that perfect distinction which is traditional among the families of France. But this majestic *ensemble* was tempered by an air of introspection and unction which gave her conversation an infinite charm, and it gained her the esteem and affection of all those who had had the good fortune to know her." She died on November 18th, 1671, only a few days after the departure for France of the apostolic vicar.

The Ursuline Convent, Quebec
Drawn on the spot by Richard Short, 1761

Her pious friend, Mother Mary of the Incarnation, first Mother Superior of the Ursulines of Quebec, soon followed her to the tomb. She expired on April 30th, 1672. In her numerous writings on the beginnings of the colony, the modesty of Mother Mary of the Incarnation has kept us in the dark concerning several important services rendered by her to New France, and many touching details of her life would not have reached us if her companion, Madame de la Peltrie, had not made them known to us. In Mother Incarnation, who merited the glorious title of the Theresa of New France, were found all the Christian virtues, but more particularly piety, patience and confidence in Providence. God was ever present and visible in her heart, acting everywhere and in everything. We see, among many other instances that might be quoted, a fine example of her enthusiasm for Heaven when, cast out of her convent in the heart of the winter by a conflagration which consumed everything, she knelt upon the snow with her Sisters, and thanked God for not having taken from them, together with their properties, their lives, which might be useful to others.

If Madame de la Peltrie and Mother Mary of the Incarnation occupy a large place in the history of Canada, it is because the institution of the Ursulines, which they founded and directed at Quebec, exercised the happiest influence on the formation of the Christian families in our country. "It was," says the Abbé Ferland, "an inestimable advantage for the country to receive from the schools maintained by the nuns, mothers of families reared in piety, familiar with their religious duties, and capable of training the hearts and minds of the new generation." It was thanks to the efforts of Madame de la Peltrie, and to the lessons of Mother Incarnation and her first co-workers, that those patriarchal families whose type still persists in our time, were formed in the early days of the colony. The same services were rendered by Sister Bourgeoys to the government of Montreal.

[7] Allusion to a verse of the poet Boileau.

[8] *History of the United States*, Vol. II., page 821.

CHAPTER XI

A TROUBLED ADMINISTRATION

A thorough study of history and the analysis of the causes and effects of great historical events prove to us that frequently men endowed with the noblest qualities have rendered only slight services to their country, because, blinded by the consciousness of their own worth, and the certainty which they have of desiring to work only for the good of their country, they have disdained too much the advice of wise counsillors. With eyes fixed upon their established purpose, they trample under foot every obstacle; and every man who differs from their opinion is but a traitor or an imbecile: hence their lack of moderation, tact and prudence, and their excess of obstinacy and violence. To select one example among a thousand, what marvellous results would have been attained by an *entente cordiale* between two men like Dupleix and La Bourdonnais.

Count de Frontenac was certainly a great man: he made Canada prosperous in peace, glorious in war, but he made also the great mistake of aiming at absolutism, and of allowing himself to be guided throughout his administration by unjustified prejudices against the Jesuits and the religious orders. Only the Sovereign Council, the bishop and the royal commissioner could have opposed his omnipotence. Now the office of commissioner remained vacant for three years, the bishop stayed in France till 1675, and his grand vicar, who was to represent him in the highest assembly of the colony, was never invited to take his seat there. As to the council, the governor took care to constitute it of men who were entirely devoted to him, and he thus made himself the arbiter of justice. The council, of which Peuvret de Mesnu was secretary, was at this time composed of MM. Le Gardeur de Tilly, Damours, de la Tesserie, Dupont, de Mouchy, and a substitute for the attorney-general.

The first difficulty which Frontenac met was brought about by a cause rather insignificant in itself, but rendered so dangerous by the obstinacy of those who were concerned in it that it caused a deep commotion throughout the whole country. Thus a foreign body, sometimes a wretched little splinter buried in the flesh, may, if we allow the wound to be poisoned, produce the greatest disorders in the human system. We cannot read without admiration of the acts of bravery and daring frequently accomplished by the *coureurs de bois*. We experience a sentiment of pride when we glance through the accounts which depict for us the endurance and physical vigour with which these athletes became endowed by dint of continual struggles with man and beast and with the very elements in a climate that was as glacial in winter as it was torrid in summer. We are happy to think that these brave and strong men belong to our race. But in the time of Frontenac the ecclesiastical and civil authorities were averse to seeing the colony lose thus the most vigorous part of its population. While admitting that the *coureurs de bois* became stout fellows in consequence of their hard experience, just as the fishermen of the French shore now become robust sailors after a few seasons of fishing on the Newfoundland Banks, the parallel is not complete, because the latter remain throughout their lives a valuable reserve for the French fleets, while the former were in great part lost to the colony, at a period when safety lay in numbers. If they escaped the manifold dangers which they ran every day in dealing with the savages in the heart of the forest, if they disdained to link themselves by the bond of marriage to a squaw and to settle among the redskins, the *coureurs de bois* were none the less drones among their compatriots; they did not make up their minds to establish themselves in places where they might have become excellent farmers, until through age and infirmity they were rather a burden than a support to others.

To counteract this scourge the king published in 1673, a decree which, under penalty of death, forbade Frenchmen to remain more than twenty-four hours in the woods without permission from the governor. Some Montreal officers, engaged in trade, violated this prohibition; the Count de Frontenac at once sent M. Bizard, lieutenant of his guards, with an order to arrest them. The governor of Montreal, M. Perrot, who connived with them, publicly insulted the officer entrusted with the orders of the governor-general. Indignant at such insolence, M. de Frontenac had M. Perrot arrested at once, imprisoned in the Château St. Louis and judged by the Sovereign Council. Connected with M. Perrot by the bonds of friendship, the Abbé de Fénelon profited by the occasion to allude, in the sermon which he delivered in the parochial church of Montreal on Easter Sunday, to the excessive labour which M. de Frontenac had exacted from the inhabitants of Ville-Marie for the erection of Fort Cataraqui. According to La Salle, who heard the sermon, the Abbé de Fénelon said: "He who is invested with authority should not disturb the people who depend on him; on the contrary, it is his duty to consider them as his children and to treat them as would a father.... He must not disturb the commerce of the country by ill-treating those who do not give him a share of the profits they may make in it; he must content himself with gaining by honest means; he must not trample on the people, nor vex them by excessive demands which serve his interests alone. He must not have favourites who praise him on all occasions, or oppress, under far-fetched pretexts, persons who serve the same princes, when they oppose his enterprises.... He has respect for priests and ministers of the Church."

Count de Frontenac felt himself directly aimed at; he was the more inclined to anger, since, the year before, he had had reasons for complaint of the sermon of a Jesuit Father. Let us allow the governor himself to relate this incident: "I had need," he wrote to Colbert, "to remember your orders on the occasion of a sermon preached by a Jesuit Father this winter (1672) purposely and without need, at which he had a week before invited everybody to be present. He gave expression in this sermon to seditious proposals against the authority of the king, which scandalized many, by dilating upon the restrictions made by the bishop of the traffic in brandy.... I was several times tempted to leave the church and to interrupt the sermon; but I eventually contented myself, after it was over, with seeking out the grand vicar and the superior of the Jesuits and telling them that I was much surprised at what I had just heard, and that I asked justice of them.... They greatly blamed the preacher, whose words they disavowed, attributing them, according to their custom, to an excess of zeal, and offered me many excuses, with which I condescended to seem satisfied, telling them, nevertheless, that I would not accept such again, and that, if the occasion ever arose, I would put the preacher where he would learn how he ought to speak...."

On the news of the words which were pronounced in the pulpit at Ville-Marie, M. de Frontenac summoned M. de Fénelon to send him a verified copy of his sermon, and on the refusal of the abbé, he cited him before the council. M. de Fénelon appeared, but objected to the jurisdiction of the court, declaring that he owed an account of his actions to the ecclesiastical authority alone. Now the official authority of the diocese was vested in the worthy M. de Bernières, the representative of Mgr. de Laval. The latter is summoned in his turn before the council, where the Count de Frontenac, who will not recognize either the authority of this official or that of the apostolic vicar, objects to M. de Bernières occupying the seat of the absent Bishop of Petræa. In order not to compromise his right thus contested, M. de Bernières replies to the questions of the council "standing and without taking any seat." The trial thus begun dragged along till autumn, to be then referred to the court of France. The superior of St. Sulpice, M. de Bretonvilliers, who had succeeded the venerable M. Olier, did not approve of the conduct of the Abbé Fénelon, for he wrote later to the Sulpicians of Montreal: "I exhort you to profit by the example of M. de Fénelon. Concerning himself too much with secular affairs and with what did not affect him, he has ruined his own cause and compromised the friends whom he wished to serve. In matters of this sort it is always best to remain neutral."

Frontenac was about to be blamed in his turn. The governor had obtained from the council a decree ordering the king's attorney to be present at the rendering of accounts by the purveyor of the

Quebec Seminary, and another decree of March 4th, 1675, declaring that not only, as had been customary since 1668, the judges should have precedence over the churchwardens in public ceremonies, but also that the latter should follow all the officers of justice; at Quebec these officers should have their bench immediately behind that of the council, and in the rest of the country, behind that of the local governors and the seigneurs. This latter decree was posted everywhere. A missionary, M. Thomas Morel, was accused of having prevented its publication at Lévis, and was arrested at once and imprisoned in the Château St. Louis with the clerk of the ecclesiastical court, Romain Becquet, who had refused to deliver to the council the registers of this ecclesiastical tribune. He was kept there a month. MM. de Bernières and Dudouyt protested, declaring that M. Morel was amenable only to the diocesan authority. We see in such an incident some of the reasons which induced Laval to insist upon the immediate constitution of a regular diocese. Summoned to produce forthwith the authority for their pretended ecclesiastical jurisdiction, "they produced a copy of the royal declaration, dated March 27th, 1659, based on the bulls of the Bishop of Petræa, and other documents, establishing incontestably the legal authority of the apostolic vicar." The council had to yield; it restored his freedom to M. Morel, and postponed until later its decision as to the validity of the claims of the ecclesiastical court.

This was a check to the ambitions of the Count de Frontenac. The following letter from Louis XIV dealt a still more cruel blow to his absolutism: "In order to punish M. Perrot for having resisted your authority," the prince wrote to him, "I have had him put into the

Bastille for some time; so that when he returns to your country, not only will this punishment render him more circumspect in his duty, but it will serve as an example to restrain others. But if I must inform you of my sentiments, after having thus satisfied my authority which was violated in your person, I will tell you that without absolute need you ought not to have these orders executed throughout the extent of a local jurisdiction like Montreal without communicating with its governor.... I have blamed the action of the Abbé de Fénelon, and have commanded him to return no more to Canada; but I must tell you that it was difficult to enter a criminal procedure against him, or to compel the priests of St. Sulpice to bear witness against him. He should have been delivered over to his bishop or to the grand vicar to suffer the ecclesiastical penalties, or should have been arrested and sent back to France by the first ship. I have been told besides," added the monarch, "that you would not permit ecclesiastics and others to attend to their missions and other duties, or even leave their residence without a passport from Montreal to Quebec; that you often summoned them for very slight causes; that you intercepted their letters and did not allow them liberty to write. If the whole or part of these things be true, you must mend your ways." On his part Colbert enjoined upon the governor a little more calmness and gentleness. "His Majesty," wrote the minister, "has ordered me to explain to you, privately, that it is absolutely necessary for the good of your service to moderate your conduct, and not to single out with too great severity faults committed either against his service or against the respect due to your person or character." Colbert rightly felt that fault-finding letters were not sufficient to keep within bounds a temperament as fiery as that of the governor of Canada; on the other hand, a man of Frontenac's worth was too valuable to the colony to think of dispensing with his services. The wisest course was to renew the Sovereign Council, and in order to withdraw its members from the too preponderant influence of the governor, to put their nomination in the hands of the king.

By the royal edict of June 5th, 1675, the council was reconstituted. It was composed of seven members appointed by the Crown; the governor-general occupied the first place, the bishop, or in his 166absence, the grand vicar, the second, and the commissioner the third. As the latter presided in the absence of the governor, and as the king was anxious that "he should have the same functions and the same privileges as the first presidents of the courts of France," as moreover the honour devolved upon him of collecting the opinions or votes and of pronouncing the decrees, it was in reality the commissioner who might be considered as actual president. It is, therefore, easy to understand the continual disputes which arose upon the question of the title of President of the Council between Frontenac and the Commissioner Jacques Duchesneau. The latter, at first "*Président des trésoriers de la généralité de Tours*," had been appointed *intendant* of New France by a commission which bears the same date as the royal edict reviving the Sovereign Council. While thinking of the material good of the colony, the Most Christian King took care not to neglect its spiritual interests; he undertook to provide for the maintenance of the parish priests and other ecclesiastics wherever necessary, and to meet in case of need the expenses of the divine service. In addition he expressed his will "that there should always be in the council one ecclesiastical member," and later he added a clerical councillor to the members already installed. There were summoned to the council MM. de Villeray, de Tilly, Damours, Dupont, Louis René de Lotbinière, de Peyras, and Denys de Vitré. M. Denis Joseph Ruette d'Auteuil was appointed solicitor-general; his functions consisted in speaking in the name of the king, and in making, in the name of the prince or of the public, the necessary statements. The former clerk, M. Peuvret de Mesnu, was retained in his functions.

The quarrels thus generated between the governor and the commissioner on the question of the title of president grew so embittered that discord did not cease to prevail between the two men on even the most insignificant questions. Forcibly involved in these dissensions, the Sovereign Council itself was divided into two hostile camps, and letters of complaint and denunciation rained upon the desk of the minister in France: on the one hand the governor was accused of receiving presents from the savages before permitting them to trade at Montreal, and was reproached for sending beavers to New England; on the other hand, it was hinted that the commissioner was interested in the business of the principal merchants of the colony. Scrupulously honest, but of a somewhat stern temperament, Duchesneau could not bend to the imperious character of Frontenac, who in his exasperation readily allowed himself to be impelled to arbitrary acts; thus he kept the councillor Damours in prison for two months for a slight cause, and banished from Quebec three other councillors, MM. de Villeray, de Tilly and d'Auteuil. The climax was reached, and in spite of the services rendered to the country by these two administrators, the king decided to recall them both in 1682.

Count de Frontenac was replaced as governor by M. Lefebvre de la Barre, and M. Duchesneau by M. de Meulles.

CHAPTER XII

THIRD VOYAGE TO FRANCE

Disembarking in the year 1675 on that soil where as apostolic vicar he had already accomplished so much good, giving his episcopal benediction to that Christian throng who came to sing the Te Deum to thank God for the happy return of their first pastor, casting his eyes upon that manly and imposing figure of one of the most illustrious lieutenants of the great king, the Count de Frontenac, what could be the thoughts of Mgr. de Laval? He could not deceive himself: the letters received from Canada proved to him too clearly that the friction between the civil powers and religious authorities would be continued under a governor of uncompromising and imperious character. With what fervour must he have asked of Heaven the tact, the prudence and the patience so necessary in such delicate circumstances!

Two questions, especially, divided the governor and the bishop: that of the permanence of livings, and the everlasting matter of the sale of brandy to the savages, a question which, like the phoenix, was continually reborn from its ashes. "The prelate," says the Abbé Gosselin, "desired to establish parishes wherever they were necessary, and procure for them good and zealous missionaries, and, as far as possible, priests residing in each district, but removable and attached to the seminary, which received the tithes and furnished them with all they had need of. But Frontenac found that this system left the priests too dependent on the bishop, and that the clergy thus closely connected with the bishop and the seminary, was too formidable and too powerful a body. It was with the purpose of weakening it and of rendering it, by the aid which it would require, more dependent on the civil authority, that he undertook that campaign for permanent livings which ended in the overthrow of Mgr. de Laval's system."

Colbert, in fact, was too strongly prejudiced against the clergy of Canada by the reports of Talon and Frontenac. These three men were wholly devoted to the interests of France as well as to those of the colony, but they judged things only from a purely human point of view. "I see," Colbert wrote in 1677 to Commissioner Duchesneau, "that the Count de Frontenac is of the opinion that the trade with the savages in drinks, called in that country intoxicating, does not cause the great and terrible evils to which Mgr. de Québec takes exception, and even that it is necessary for commerce; and I see that you are of an opinion contrary to this. In this matter, before taking sides with the bishop, you should enquire very exactly as to the number of murders, assassinations, cases of arson, and other excesses caused by brandy ... and send me the proof of this. If these deeds had been continual, His Majesty would have issued a most severe and vigorous prohibition to all his subjects against engaging in this traffic. But, in the absence of this proof, and seeing, moreover, the contrary in the evidence and reports of those that have been longest in this country, it is not just, and the general policy of a state opposes in this the feelings of a bishop who, to prevent the abuses that a small number of private individuals may make of a thing good in itself, wishes to abolish trade in an article which greatly serves to attract commerce, and the savages themselves, to the orthodox Christians." Thus M. Dudouyt could not but fail in his mission, and he wrote to Mgr. de Laval that Colbert, while recognizing very frankly the devotion of the bishop and the missionaries, believed that they exaggerated the fatal results of the traffic. The zealous collaborator of the Bishop of Quebec at the same time urged the prelate to suspend the spiritual penalties till then imposed upon the traders, in order to deprive the minister of every motive of bitterness against the clergy.

The bishop admitted the wisdom of this counsel, which he followed, and meanwhile the king, alarmed by a report from Commissioner Duchesneau, who shared the view of the missionaries, desired to investigate and come to a final decision on the question. He therefore ordered the Count de Frontenac to choose in the colony twenty-four competent persons, and to commission them to examine the drawbacks to the sale of intoxicating liquors. Unfortunately, the persons chosen for this enquiry were engaged in trade with the savages; their conclusions must necessarily be prejudiced. They declared that "very few disorders arose from the traffic in brandy, among the natives of the country; that, moreover, the Dutch, by distributing intoxicating drinks to the Iroquois, attracted by this means the trade in beaver skins to Orange and Manhattan. It was, therefore, absolutely necessary to allow the brandy trade in order to bring the savages into the French colony and to prevent them from taking their furs to foreigners."

We cannot help being surprised at such a judgment when we read over the memoirs of the time, which all agree in deploring the sad results of this traffic. The most crying injustice, the most revolting immorality, the ruin of families, settlements devastated by drunkenness, agriculture abandoned, the robust portion of the population ruining its health in profitless expeditions: such were some of the most horrible fruits of alcohol. And what do we find as a compensation for so many evils? A few dozen rascals enriched, returning to squander in France a fortune shamefully acquired. And let it not be objected that, if the Indians had not been able to purchase the wherewithal to satisfy their terrible passion for strong drink, they would have carried their furs to the English or the Dutch, for it was proven that the offer of Governor Andros, to forbid the sale of brandy to the savages in New England on condition that the French would act likewise in New France, was formally rejected. "To-day when the passions of the time have long been silent," says the Abbé Ferland, "it is impossible not to admire the energy displayed by the noble bishop, imploring the pity of the monarch for the savages of New France with all the courage shown by Las Casas, when he pleaded the cause of the aborigines of Spanish America. Disdaining the hypocritical outcries of those men who prostituted the name of commerce to cover their speculations and their rapine, he exposed himself to scorn and persecution in order to save the remnant of those indigenous American tribes, to protect his flock from the moral contagion which threatened to weigh upon it, and to lead into the right path the young men who were going to ruin among the savage tribes."

The worthy bishop desired to prevent the laxity of the sale of brandy that might result from the declaration of the Committee of Twenty-four, and in the autumn of 1678 he set out again for France. To avoid a journey so fatiguing, he might easily have found excuses in the rest needed after a difficult pastoral expedition which he had just concluded, in the labours of his seminary which demanded his presence, and especially in the bad state of his health; but is not the first duty of a leader always to stand in the breach, and to give to all the example of self-sacrifice? A report from his hand on the disorders caused by the traffic in strong liquors would perhaps have obtained a fortunate result, but thinking that his presence at the court would be still more efficacious, he set out. He managed to find in his charity and the goodness of his heart such eloquent words to depict the evils wrought upon the Church in Canada by the scourge of intoxication, that Louis XIV was moved, and commissioned his confessor, Father La Chaise, to examine the question conjointly with the Archbishop of Paris. According to their advice, the king expressly forbade the French to carry intoxicating liquors to the savages in their dwellings or in the woods, and he wrote to Frontenac to charge him to see that the edict was respected. On his part, Laval consented to maintain the *cas réservé* only against those who might infringe the royal prohibition. The Bishop of Quebec had hoped for more; for nothing could prevent the Indians from coming to buy the terrible poison from the French, and moreover, discovery of the infractions of the law would be, if not impossible, at least most difficult. Nevertheless, it was an advantage obtained over the dealers and their protectors, who aimed at nothing less than an unrestricted traffic in brandy. A dyke was set up against the devastations of the scourge; the worthy bishop might hope to maintain it energetically by his vigilance and that of his coadjutors. Unfortunately, he could not succeed entirely, and little by little the disorders became so multiplied that M. de Denonville considered brandy as one of the greatest evils of Canada, and that the venerable superior of St. Sulpice de Montréal, M. Dollier de Casson, wrote in 1691: "I have been twenty-six years in this country, and I have seen our numerous and flourishing Algonquin missions all destroyed by drunkenness." Accordingly, it became necessary later to fall back upon the former rigorous regulations against the sale of intoxicating liquors to the Indians.

Before his departure for France the Bishop of Quebec had given the devoted priests of St. Sulpice a mark of his affection: he constituted the parish of Notre-Dame de Montréal according to the canons of the Church, and joined it in perpetuity to the Seminary of Ville-Marie, "to be administered, under the plenary authority of the Bishops of Quebec, by such ecclesiastics as might be chosen by the superior of the said seminary. The priests of St. Sulpice having by their efforts and their labours produced during so many years in New France, and especially in the Island of Montreal, very great fruits for the glory of God and the advantage of this growing Church, we have given them, as being most irreproachable in faith, doctrine, piety and conduct, in perpetuity, and do give them, by virtue of these presents, the livings of the Island of Montreal, in order that they may be perfectly cultivated as up to now they have been, as best they might be by their preachings and examples." In fact, misunderstandings like that which had occurred on the arrival of de Queylus were no longer to be feared; since the authority to which Laval could lay claim had been duly established and proved, the Sulpicians had submitted and accepted his jurisdiction. They had for a longer period preserved their independence as temporal lords, and the governor of Ville-Marie, de Maisonneuve, jealous of preserving intact the rights of those whom he represented, even dared one day to refuse the keys of the fort to the governor-general, M. d'Argenson. Poor de Maisonneuve paid for this excessive zeal by the loss of his position, for d'Argenson never forgave him.

The parish of Notre-Dame was united with the Seminary of Montreal on October 30th, 1678, one year after the issuing of the letters patent which recognized the civil existence of St. Sulpice de Montréal. Mgr. de Laval at the same time united with the parish of Notre-Dame the chapel of Bonsecours. On the banks of the St. Lawrence, not far from the church of Notre-Dame, rises a chapel of modest appearance. It is Notre-Dame de Bonsecours. It has seen many generations kneeling on its square, and has not ceased to protect with its shadow the Catholic quarter of Montreal. The buildings about it rose successively, only to give way themselves to other monuments. Notre-Dame de Bonsecours is still respected; the piety of Catholics defends it against all attacks of time or progress, and the little church raises proudly in the air that slight wooden steeple that more than once has turned aside the avenging bolt of the Most High. Sister Bourgeoys had begun it in 1657; to obtain the funds necessary for its completion she betook herself to Paris. She obtained one hundred francs from M. Macé, a priest of St. Sulpice. One of the associates of the Company of Montreal, M. de Fancamp, received for her from two of his fellow-partners, MM. Denis and Leprêtre, a statuette of the Virgin made of the miraculous wood of Montagu, and he himself, to participate in this gift, gave her a shrine of the most wonderful richness to contain the precious statue. On her return to Canada, Marguerite Bourgeoys caused to be erected near the house of the Sisters a wooden lean-to in the form of a chapel, which became the provisional sanctuary of the statuette. Two years later, on June 29th, the laying of the foundation stone of the chapel took place. The work was urged with enthusiasm, and encouraged by the pious impatience of Sister Bourgeoys. The generosity of the faithful vied in enthusiasm, and gifts flowed in. M. de Maisonneuve offered a cannon, of which M. Souart had a bell made at his expense. Two thousand francs, furnished by the piety of the inhabitants, and one hundred louis from Sister Bourgeoys and her nuns, aided the foundress to complete the realization of a wish long cherished in her heart; the new chapel became an inseparable annex of the parish of Ville-Marie.

These most precious advantages were recognized on November 6th, 1678, by Mgr. de Laval, who preserved throughout his life the most tender devotion to the Mother of God. On the other hand, the prelate imposed upon the parish priest the obligation of having the Holy Mass celebrated there on the Day of the Visitation, and of going there in procession on the Day of the Assumption. Is it necessary to mention with what zeal, with what devotion the Canadians brought to Mary in this new temple their homage and their prayers? Let us listen to the enthusiastic narrative of Sister Morin, a nun of St. Joseph: "The Holy Mass is said there every day, and even several times a day, to satisfy the devotion and the trust of the people, which are great towards Notre-Dame de Bonsecours. Processions wend their way thither on occasions of public need or calamity, with much success. It is the regular promenade of the devout persons of the town, who make a pilgrimage there every evening, and there are few good Catholics who, from all the places in Canada, do not make vows of offerings to this chapel in all the dangers in which they find themselves."

The church of Notre-Dame de Bonsecours was twice remodelled; built at first of oak on stone foundations, it was rebuilt of stone and consumed in 1754 in a conflagration which destroyed a part of the town. In 1772 the chapel was rebuilt as it exists now, one hundred and two feet long by forty-six wide.

CHAPTER XIII

LAVAL RETURNS TO CANADA

Mgr. de Laval was still in France when the edict of May, 1679, appeared, decreeing on the suggestion of Frontenac, that the tithe should be paid only to "each of the parish priests within the extent of his parish where he is established in perpetuity in the stead of the removable priest who previously administered it." The ideas of the Count de Frontenac were thus victorious, and the king retracted his first decision. He had in his original decree establishing the Seminary of Quebec, granted the bishop and his successors "the right of recalling and displacing the priests by them delegated to the parishes to exercise therein parochial functions." Laval on his return to Canada conformed without murmur to the king's decision; he worked, together with the governor and commissioner, at drawing up the plan of the parishes to be established, and sent his vicar-general to install the priests who were appointed to the different livings. He desired to inspire his whole clergy with the disinterestedness which he had always evinced, for not only did he recommend his priests "to content themselves with the simplest living, and with the bare necessaries of their support," but besides, agreeing with the governor and the commissioner, he estimated that an annual sum of five hundred livres merely, that is to say, about three hundred dollars of our present money, was sufficient for the lodging and maintenance of a priest. This was more than modest, and yet, without a very considerable extension, there was no parish capable of supplying the needs of its priest. There was indeed, it is true, an article of the edict specifying that in case of the tithe being insufficient, the necessary supplement should be fixed by the council and furnished by the seigneur of the place and by the inhabitants; but this manner of aiding the priests who were reduced to a bare competence was not practical, as was soon evident. Another article gave the title of patron to any seigneur who should erect a religious edifice; this article was just as fantastic, "for," wrote Commissioner Duchesneau, "there is no private person in this country who is in a position to build churches of any kind."

The king, always well disposed towards the clergy of Canada, came to their aid again in this matter. He granted them an annual income of eight thousand francs, to be raised from his "Western Dominions," that is to say, from the sum derived in Canada from the *droit du quart* and the farm of Tadousac; from these funds, which were distributed by the seminary until 1692, and after this date by the bishop alone, two thousand francs were to be set aside for priests prevented by illness or old age from fulfilling the duties of the holy ministry, and twelve hundred francs were to be employed in the erection of parochial churches. This aid came aptly, but was not sufficient, as Commissioner de Beauharnois himself admits. And yet the deplorable state in which the treasury of France then was, on account of the enormous expenses indulged in by Louis XIV, and especially in consequence of the wars which he waged against Europe, obliged him to diminish this allowance. In 1707 it was reduced by half.

It was feared for a time by the Sulpicians that the edict of 1679 might injure the rights which they had acquired from the union with their seminary of the parishes established on the Island of

Montreal, and they therefore hastened to request from the king the civil confirmation of this canonical union. "There is," they said in their request, "a sort of need that the parishes of the Island of Montreal and of the surrounding parts should be connected with a community able to furnish them with priests, who could not otherwise be found in the country, to administer the said livings; these priests would not expose themselves to a sea voyage and to leaving their family comforts to go and sacrifice themselves in a wild country, if they did not hope that in their infirmity or old age they would be free to withdraw from the laborious administration of the parishes, and that they would find a refuge in which to end their days in tranquillity in a community which, on its part, would not pledge itself in such a way as to afford them the hope of this refuge, and to furnish other priests in their place, if it had not the free control of the said parishes and power to distribute among them the ecclesiastics belonging to its body whom it might judge capable of this, and withdraw or exchange them when fitting." The request of the Sulpicians was granted by the king.

It was not until 1680 that the Bishop of Quebec could return to Canada. The all-important questions of the permanence of livings and of the traffic in brandy were not the only ones which kept him in France; another difficulty, that of the dependence of his diocese, demanded of his devotion a great many efforts at the court. The circumstances were difficult. France was plunged at this period in the famous dispute between the government and the court of Rome over the question of the right of *régale*, a dispute which nearly brought about a schism. The Archbishop of Paris,

Mgr. de Harlay, who had laboured so much when he was Bishop of Rouen to keep New France under the jurisdiction of the diocese of Normandy, used his influence to make Canada dependent on the archbishopric of Paris. The death of this prelate put an end to this claim, and the French colony in North America continued its direct connection with the Holy See.

Mgr. de Laval strove also to obtain from the Holy Father the canonical union of the abbeys of Maubec and of Lestrées with his bishopric; if he had obtained it, he could have erected his chapter at once, assuring by the revenues of these monasteries a sufficient maintenance for his canons. The opposition of the religious orders on which these abbeys depended defeated his plan, but in compensation he obtained from the generosity of the king a grant of land on which his successor, Saint-Vallier, afterwards erected the church of Notre-Dame des Victoires. The venerable prelate might well ask favours for his diocese when he himself set an example of the greatest generosity. By a deed, dated at Paris, he gave to his seminary all that he possessed: Ile Jésus, the seigniories of Beaupré and Petite Nation, a property at Château Richer, finally books, furniture, funds, and all that might belong to him at the moment of his death.

Laval returned to Canada at a time when the relations with the savage tribes were becoming so strained as to threaten an impending rupture. So far had matters gone that Colonel Thomas Dongan, governor of New York, had urged the Iroquois to dig up the hatchet, and he was only too willingly obeyed. Unfortunately, the two governing heads of the colony were replaced just at that moment. Governor de Frontenac and Commissioner Duchesneau

155

were recalled in 1682, and supplanted by de la Barre and de Meulles. The latter were far from equalling their predecessors. M. de Lefebvre de la Barre was a clever sailor but a deplorable administrator; as for the commissioner, M. de Meulles, his incapacity did not lessen his extreme conceit.

On his arrival at Quebec, Laval learned with deep grief that a terrible conflagration had, a few weeks before, consumed almost the whole of the Lower Town. The houses, and even the stores being then built of wood, everything was devoured by the flames. A single dwelling escaped the disaster, that of a rich private person, M. Aubert de la Chesnaie, in whose house mass was said every Sunday and feast-day for the citizens of the Lower Town who could not go to the parish service. To bear witness of his gratitude to Heaven, M. de la Chesnaie came to the aid of a good number of his fellow-citizens, and helped them with his money to rebuild their houses. This fire injured the merchants of Montreal almost as much as those of Quebec, and the *Histoire de l'Hôtel-Dieu* relates that "more riches were lost on that sad night than all Canada now possesses."

The king had the greatest desire for the future reign of harmony in the colony; accordingly he enjoined upon M. de Meulles to use every effort to agree with the governor-general: "If the latter should fail in his duty to the sovereign, the commissioner should content himself with a remonstrance and allow him to act further without disturbing him, but as soon as possible afterwards should render an account to the king's council of what might be prejudicial to the good of the state." Mgr. de Laval, to whom the prince had written in the same tenor, replied at once: "The honour which your

Majesty has done me in writing to me that M. de Meulles has orders to preserve here a perfect understanding with me in all things, and to give me all the aid in his power, is so evident a mark of the affection which your Majesty cherishes for this new Church and for the bishop who governs it, that I feel obliged to assure your Majesty of my most humble gratitude. As I do not doubt that this new commissioner whom you have chosen will fulfil with pleasure your commands, I may also assure your Majesty that on my part I shall correspond with him in the fulfilment of my duty, and that I shall all my life consider it my greatest joy to enter into the intentions of your Majesty for the general good of this country, which constitutes a part of your dominions." Concord thus advised could not displease a pastor who loved nothing so much as union and harmony among all who held the reins of power, a pastor who had succeeded in making his Church a family so united that it was quoted once as a model in one of the pulpits of Paris. If he sometimes strove against the powerful of this earth, it was when it was a question of combating injustice or some abuse prejudicial to the welfare of his flock. "Although by his superior intelligence," says Latour, "by his experience, his labours, his virtues, his birth and his dignity, he was an oracle whose views the whole clergy respected, no one ever more distrusted himself, or asked with more humility, or followed with more docility the counsel of his inferiors and disciples.... He was less a superior than a colleague, who sought the right with them and sought it only for its own sake. Accordingly, never was prelate better obeyed or better seconded than Mgr. de Laval, because, far from having that professional jealousy which desires to do everything itself, which dreads merit and enjoys only despotism, never did prelate evince more appreciative confidence in his inferiors, or seek more earnestly to give zeal and talent their dues, or have less desire to command, or did, in fact, command less." The new governor brought from France strong prejudices against the bishop; he lost them very quickly, and he wrote to the minister, the Marquis de Seignelay: "We have greatly laboured, the bishop and I, in the establishment of the parishes of this country. I send you the arrangement which we have arrived at concerning them. We owe it to the bishop, who is extremely well affected to the country, and in whom we must trust." The minister wrote to the prelate and expressed to him his entire satisfaction in his course.

The vigilant bishop had not yet entirely recovered from the fatigue of his journey when he decided, in spite of the infirmities which were beginning to overwhelm him, and which were to remain the constant companions of his latest years, to visit all the parishes and the religious communities of his immense diocese. He had already traversed them in the winter time in his former pastoral visits, shod with snowshoes, braving the fogs, the snow and the bitterest weather. In the suffocating heat of summer, travel in a bark canoe was scarcely less fatiguing to a man of almost sixty years, worn out by the hard ministry of a quarter of a century. However, he decided on a summer journey, and set out on June 1st, 1681, accompanied by M. de Maizerets, one of his grand vicars. He visited successively Lotbinière, Batiscan, Champlain, Cap-de-la-Madeleine, Trois Rivières, Chambly, Sorel, St. Ours, Contrecœur, Verchères, Boucherville, Repentigny, Lachesnaie, and arrived on June 19th at Montreal. The marks of respectful affection lavished upon him by the population compel him to receive continual visits; but he has come especially for his beloved religious communities, and he honours them all with his presence, the Seminary of St. Sulpice as well as the Congregation of Notre-Dame and the hospital. These labours are not sufficient for his apostolic zeal; he betakes himself to the house of the Jesuit Fathers at Laprairie, then to their Indian Mission at the Sault St. Louis, finally to the parish of St. François de Sales, in the Ile Jésus. Descending the St. Lawrence River, he sojourns successively at Longueuil, at Varennes, at Lavaltrie, at Nicolet, at Bécancourt, at Gentilly, at Ste. Anne de la Pérade, at Deschambault. He returns to Quebec; his devoted fellow-workers in the seminary urge him to rest, but he will think of rest only when his mission is fully ended. He sets out again, and Ile aux Oies, Cap-Saint-Ignace, St. Thomas, St. Michel, Beaumont, St. Joseph de Lévis have in turn the happiness of receiving their pastor. The undertaking was too great for the bishop's strength, and he suffered the results which could not but follow upon such a strain. The registers of the Sovereign Council prove to us that only a week after his return he had to take to his bed, and for two months could not occupy his seat among the other councillors. "His Lordship fell ill of a dangerous malady," says a memoir of that time. "For the space of a fortnight his death was expected, but God granted us the favour of bringing him to convalescence, and eventually to his former health."

M. de la Barre, on his arrival, desired to inform himself exactly of the condition of the colony. In a great assembly held at Quebec, on October 10th, 1682, he gathered all the men who occupied positions of consideration in the colony. Besides the governor, the bishop and the commissioner, there were noticed among others M. Dollier de Casson, the superior of the Seminary of St. Sulpice at Montreal, several Jesuit Fathers, MM. de Varennes, governor of Three Rivers, d'Ailleboust, de Brussy and Le Moyne. The information which M. de la Barre obtained from the assembly was far from reassuring; incessantly stirred up by Governor Dongan's genius for intrigue, the Iroquois were preparing to descend upon the little colony. If they had not already begun hostilities, it was because they wished first to massacre the tribes allied with the French; already the Hurons, the Algonquins, the Conestogas, the Delawares and a portion of the Illinois had fallen under their blows. It was necessary to save from extermination the Ottawa and Illinois tribes. Now, one might indeed raise a thousand robust men, accustomed to savage warfare, but, if they were used for an expedition, who would cultivate in their absence the lands of these brave men? A prompt reinforcement from the mother country became urgent, and M. de la Barre hastened to demand it.

The war had already begun. The Iroquois had seized two canoes, the property of La Salle, near Niagara; they had likewise attacked and plundered fourteen Frenchmen en route to the Illinois with merchandise valued at sixteen thousand francs. It was known, besides, that the Cayugas and the Senecas were preparing to attack the French settlements the following summer. In spite of all, the expected help did not arrive. One realizes the anguish to which the population must have been a prey when one reads the following letter from the Bishop of Quebec: "Sire, the Marquis de Seignelay will inform your Majesty of the war which the Iroquois have declared against your subjects of New France, and will explain the need of sending aid sufficient to destroy, if possible, this enemy, who has opposed for so many years the establishment of this colony.... Since it has pleased your Majesty to choose me for the government of this growing Church, I feel obliged, more than any one, to make its needs manifest to you. The paternal care which you have always had for us leaves me no room to doubt that you will give the necessary orders for the most prompt aid possible, without which this poor country would be exposed to a danger nigh unto ruin."

The expected reinforcements finally arrived; on November 9th, 1684, the whole population of Quebec, assembled at the harbour, received with joy three companies of soldiers, composed of fifty-two men each. The Bishop of Quebec did not fail to express to the king his personal obligation and the gratitude of all: "The troops which your Majesty has sent to defend us against the Iroquois," he wrote to the king, "and the lands which you have granted us for the subsidiary church of the Lower Town, and the funds which you have allotted both to rebuild the cathedral spire and to aid in the maintenance of the priests, these are favours which oblige me to thank your Majesty, and make me hope that you will deign to continue your royal bounties to our Church and the whole colony."

M. de la Barre was thus finally able to set out on his expedition against the Iroquois. At the head of one hundred and thirty soldiers, seven hundred militia and two hundred and sixty Indians, he marched to Lake Ontario, where the Iroquois, intimidated, sent him a deputation. The ambassadors, who expected to see a brilliant army full of ardour, were astonished to find themselves in the presence of pale and emaciated soldiers, worn out more by sickness and privations of every kind than by fatigue. The governor, in fact, had lost ten or twelve days at Montreal; on the way the provisions had become spoiled and insufficient, hence the name of Famine Creek given to the place where he entered with his troops, above the Oswego River. At this sight the temper of the delegates changed, and their proposals showed it; they spoke with arrogance, and almost demanded peace; they undertook to indemnify the French merchants plundered by them on condition that the army should decamp on the morrow. Such weakness could not attract to M. de la Barre the affection of the colonists; the king relieved him from his functions, and appointed as his successor the Marquis de Denonville, a colonel of dragoons, whose valour seemed to promise the colony better days.

CHAPTER XIV

RESIGNATION OF MGR. DE LAVAL

The long and conscientious pastoral visit which he had just ended had proved to the indefatigable prelate that it would be extremely difficult to establish his parishes solidly. Instead of grouping themselves together, which would have given them the advantages of union both against the attacks of savages and for the circumstances of life in which man has need of the aid of his fellows, the colonists had built their dwellings at random, according to the inspiration of the moment, and sometimes at long distances from each other; thus there existed, as late as 1678, only twenty-five fixed livings, and it promised to be very difficult to found new ones. To give a pastor the direction of parishioners established within an enormous radius of his parish house, was to condemn his ministry in advance to inefficacy. To prove it, the Abbé Gosselin cites a striking example. Of the two missionaries who shared the southern shore, the one, M. Morel, ministered to the country between Berthier and Rivière du Loup; the other, M. Volant de Saint-Claude, from Berthier to Rivière du Chêne, and each of them had only about sixty families scattered here and there. And how was one to expect that these poor farmers could maintain their pastor and build a church? Almost everywhere the chapels were of wood or clapboards, and thatched; not more than eight or nine centres of population could boast of possessing a stone church; many hamlets still lacked a chapel and imitated the Lower Town of Quebec, whose inhabitants attended service in a private house. As to priests' houses, they were a luxury that few villages could afford: the priest had to content himself with being sheltered by a respectable colonist.

During the few weeks when illness confined him to his bed, Laval had leisure to reflect on the difficulties of his task. He understood that his age and the infirmities which the Lord laid upon him would no longer permit him to bring to so arduous a work the necessary energy. "His humility," says Sister Juchereau, "persuaded him that another in his place would do more good than he, although he really did a great deal, because he sought only the glory of God and the welfare of his flock." In consequence, he decided to go and carry in person his resignation to the king. But before embarking for France, with his accustomed prudence he set his affairs in order. He had one plan, especially, at heart, that of establishing according to the rules of the Church the chapter which had already existed *de facto* for a long while. Canons are necessary to a bishopric; their duties are not merely decorative, for they assist the bishop in his episcopal office, form his natural council, replace him on certain occasions, govern the diocese from the death of its head until the deceased is replaced, and finally officiate in turn before the altars of the cathedral in order that prayer shall incessantly ascend from the diocese towards the Most High. The only obstacle to this creation until now had been the lack of resources, for the canonical union with the abbeys of Maubec and Lestrées was not yet an accomplished fact. Mgr. de Laval resolved to appeal to the unselfishness of the priests of the seminary, and he succeeded: they consented to fulfil without extra salary the duties of canons.

By an ordinance of November 6th, 1684, the Bishop of Quebec established a chapter composed of twelve canons and four chaplains. The former, among whom were five priests born in the colony, were M. Henri de Bernières, priest of Quebec, who remained dean until his death in 1700; MM. Louis Ange de Maizerets, archdeacon, Charles Glandelet, theologist, Dudouyt, grand cantor, and Jean Gauthier de Brulon, confessor. The ceremony of installation took place with the greatest pomp, amid the boom of artillery and the joyful sound of bells and music; governor, intendant, councillors, officers and soldiers, inhabitants of the city and the environments, everybody wished to be present. It remained to give a constitution to the new chapter. Mgr. de Laval had already busied himself with this for several months, and corresponded on this subject with M. Chéron, a clever lawyer of Paris. Accordingly, the constitution which he submitted for the infant chapter on the very morrow of the ceremony was admired unreservedly and adopted without discussion. Twenty-four hours afterwards he set sail accompanied by the good wishes of his priests, who, with anxious heart and tears in their eyes, followed him with straining gaze until the vessel disappeared below the horizon. Before his departure, he had, like a father who in his last hour divides his goods among his children, given his seminary a new proof of his attachment: he left it a sum of eight thousand francs for the building of the chapel.

It would seem that sad presentiments assailed him at this moment, for he said in the deed of gift: "I declare that my last will is to be buried in this chapel; and if our Lord disposes of my life during this voyage I desire that my body be brought here for

burial. I also desire this chapel to be open to the public."
Fortunately, he was mistaken, it was not the intention of the Lord
to remove him so soon from the affections of his people. For twenty
years more the revered prelate was to spread about him good works
and good examples, and Providence reserved for him the happiness
of dying in the midst of his flock.

His generosity did not confine itself to this grant. He could not
leave his diocese, which he was not sure of seeing again, without
giving a token of remembrance to that school of St. Joachim,
which he had founded and which he loved so well; he gave the
seminary eight thousand francs for the support of the priest
entrusted with the direction of the school at the same time as with
the ministry of the parish, and another sum of four thousand
francs to build the village church.

A young Canadian priest, M. Guyon, son of a farmer of the
Beaupré shore, had the good fortune of accompanying the bishop
on the voyage. It would have been very imprudent to leave the
venerable prelate alone, worn out as he was by troublesome fits of
vertigo whenever he indulged too long in work; besides, he was
attacked by a disease of the heart, whose onslaughts sometimes
incapacitated him.

It would be misjudging the foresight of Mgr. de Laval to think
that before embarking for the mother country he had not sought
out a priest worthy to replace him. He appealed to two men whose
judgment and circumspection he esteemed, M. Dudouyt and
Father Le Valois of the Society of Jesus. He asked them to
recommend a true servant of God, virtuous and zealous above all.

Father Le Valois indicated the Abbé Jean Baptiste de la Croix de Saint-Vallier, the king's almoner, whose zeal for the welfare of souls, whose charity, great piety, modesty and method made him the admiration of all. The influence which his position and the powerful relations of his family must gain for the Church in Canada were an additional argument in his favour; the superior of St. Sulpice, M. Tronson, who was also consulted, praised highly the talents and the qualities of the young priest. "My Lord has shown great virtue in his resignation," writes M. Dudouyt. "I know no occasion on which he has shown so strongly his love for his Church; for he has done everything that could be desired to procure a person capable of preserving and perfecting the good work which he has begun here." If the Abbé de Saint-Vallier had not been a man after God's own heart, he would not have accepted a duty so honourable but so difficult. He was not unaware of the difficulties which he would have to surmount, for Mgr. de Laval explained them to him himself with the greatest frankness; and, what was a still greater sacrifice, the king's almoner was to leave the most brilliant court in the world for a very remote country, still in process of organization. Nevertheless he accepted, and Laval had the satisfaction of knowing that he was committing his charge into the hands of a worthy successor.

It was now only a question of obtaining the consent of the king before petitioning the sovereign pontiff for the canonical establishment of the new episcopal authority. It was not without difficulty that it was obtained, for the prince could not decide to accept the resignation of a prelate who seemed to him indispensable to the interests of New France. He finally understood that the decision of Mgr. de Laval was irrevocable; as a mark of confidence and esteem he allowed him to choose his successor.

At this period the misunderstanding created between the common father of the faithful and his most Christian Majesty by the claims of the latter in the matter of the right of *régale* kept the Church in a false position, to the grief of all good Catholics. Pope Innocent XI waited with persistent and calm firmness until Louis XIV should become again the elder son of the Church; until then France could not exist for him, and more than thirty episcopal sees remained without occupants in the country of Saint Louis and of Joan of Arc. It was not, then, to be hoped that the appointment by the king of the Abbé de Saint-Vallier as second bishop of Quebec could be immediately sanctioned by the sovereign pontiff. It was decided that Mgr. de Laval, to whom the king granted an annuity for life of two thousand francs from the revenues of the bishopric of Aire, should remain titular bishop until the consecration of his successor, and that M. de Saint-Vallier, appointed provisionally grand vicar of the prelate, should set out immediately for New France, where he would assume the government of the diocese. The Abbé de Saint-Vallier had not yet departed before he gaveevidence of his munificence, and proved to the faithful of his future bishopric that he would be to them as generous a father as he whom he was about to replace. By deed of May 10th, 1685, he presented to the Seminary of Quebec a sum of forty-two thousand francs, to be used for the maintenance of missionaries; he bequeathed to it at the same time all the furniture, books, etc., which he should possess at his death. Laval's purpose was to remain for the present in France, where he would busy himself actively for the interests of Canada, but his fixed resolve was to go and end his days on that soil of New France which he loved so well. It was in 1688, only a few months after the official appointment of Saint-Vallier to the bishopric of Quebec, and his consecration on January 25th of the same year, that Laval returned to Canada.

M. de Saint-Vallier embarked at La Rochelle in the beginning of June, 1685, on the royal vessel which was carrying to Canada the new governor-general, M. de Denonville. The king having permitted him to take with him a score of persons, he made a most judicious choice: nine ecclesiastics, several school-masters and a few good workmen destined for the labours of the seminary, accompanied him. The voyage was long and very fatiguing. The passengers were, however, less tried than those of two other ships which followed them, on one of which more than five hundred soldiers had been crowded together. As might have been expected, sickness was not long in breaking out among them; more than one hundred and fifty of these unfortunates died, and their bodies were cast into the sea.

Immediately after his arrival the grand vicar visited all the religious establishments of the town, and he observed everywhere so much harmony and good spirit that he could not pass it over in silence. Speaking with admiration of the seminary, he said: "Every one in it devoted himself to spiritual meditation, with such blessed results that from the youngest cleric to the highest ecclesiastics in holy orders each one brought of his own accord all his personal possessions to be used in common. It seemed to me then that I saw revived in the Church of Canada something of that spirit of unworldliness which constituted one of the principal beauties of the budding Church of Jerusalem in the time of the apostles." The examples of brotherly unity and self-effacement which he admired so much in others he also set himself: he placed in the library of the seminary a magnificent collection of books which he had brought with him, and deposited in the coffers of the house several thousand francs in money, his personal property. Braving the rigours of the season, he set out in the winter of 1685 and visited the shore of Beaupré, the Island of Orleans, and then the north shore as far as Montreal. In the spring he took another direction, and inspected all the missions of Gaspesia and Acadia. He was so well satisfied with the condition of his diocese that he wrote to Mgr. de Laval: "All that I regret is that there is no more good for me to do in this Church."

In the spring of this same year, 1686, a valiant little troop was making a more warlike pastoral visit. To seventy robust Canadians, commanded by d'Iberville, de Sainte-Hélène and de Maricourt, all sons of Charles Le Moyne, the governor had added thirty good soldiers under the orders of MM. de Troyes, Duchesnil and Catalogne, to take part in an expedition for the capture of Hudson Bay from the English. Setting out on snowshoes, dragging their provisions and equipment on toboggans, then advancing, sometimes on foot, sometimes in bark canoes, they penetrated by the Ottawa River and Temiskaming and Abitibi Lakes as far as James Bay. They did not brave so many dangers and trials without being resolved to conquer or die; accordingly, in spite of its twelve cannon, Fort Monsipi was quickly carried.

The two forts, Rupert and Ste. Anne, suffered the same fate, and the only one that remained to the English, that named Fort Nelson, was preserved to them solely because its remote situation saved it. The head of the expedition, M. de Troyes, on his return to Quebec, rendered an account of his successes to M. de Denonville and to a new commissioner, M. de Champigny, who had just replaced M. de Meulles.

The bishop's infirmities left him scarcely any respite. "My health," he wrote to his successor, "is exceedingly good considering the bad use I make of it. It seems, however, that the wound which I had in my foot during five or six months at Quebec has been for the last three weeks threatening to re-open. The holy will of God be done!" And he added, in his firm resolution to pass his last days in Canada: "In any case, I feel that I have sufficient strength and health to return this year to the only place which now can give me peace and rest. *In pace in idipsum dormiam et requiescam.* Meanwhile, as we must have no other aim than the good pleasure of our Lord, whatever desire He gives me for this rest and peace, He grants me at the same time the favour of making Him a sacrifice of it in submitting myself to the opinion that you have expressed, that I should stay this year in France, to be present at your return next autumn." The bad state of his health did not prevent him from devoting his every moment to Canadian interests. He went into the most infinitesimal details of the administration of his diocese, so great was his solicitude for his work. "We must hasten this year, if possible," he wrote, "to labour at the re-establishment of the church of Ste. Anne du Petit-Cap, to which the whole country has such an attachment. We must work also to push forward the clearing of the lands of St. Joachim, in order that we may have the proper rotation crops on each farm, and that the farms may suffice for the needs of the seminary." In another letter he concerns himself with the sum of three thousand francs granted by the king each year for the marriage portion of a certain number of poor young girls marrying in Canada. "We should," says he, "distribute these moneys in parcels, fifty francs, or ten crowns, to the numerous poor families scattered along the shores, in which there is a large number of children." He practises this wise economy constantly when it is a question, not of his personal property, but of the funds of his seminary. He finds that his successor, whom the ten years which he had passed at court as king's almoner could not have trained in parsimony, allows himself to be carried away, by his zeal and his desire to do good, to a somewhat excessive expense. With what tact and delicacy he indulges in a discreet reproach! "*Magna est fides tua*," he writes to him, "and much greater than mine. We see that all our priests have responded to it with the same confidence and entire submission with which they have believed it their duty to meet your sentiments, in which they have my approval. My particular admiration has been aroused by seeing in all your letters and in all the impulses of your heart so great a reliance on the lovable Providence of God that not only has it permitted you not to have the least doubt that it would abundantly provide the wherewithal for the support of all the works which it has suggested to you, but that upon this basis, which is the firm truth, you have had the courage to proceed to the execution of them. It is true that my heart has long yearned for what you have accomplished; but I have never had sufficient confidence or reliance to undertake it. I always awaited the means *quæ pater posuit in suâ potestate*. I hope that, since the Most Holy Family of our Lord has suggested all these works to you, they will give you means and ways to maintain what is so much to the glory of God and the welfare of souls. But, according to all appearances, great difficulties will be found, which will only serve to increase this confidence and trust in God." And he ends with this prudent advice: "Whatever confidence God desires us to have in His providence, it is certain that He demands from us the observance of rules of prudence, not human and political, but Christian and just."

He concerns himself even with the servants, and it is singular to note that his mind, so apt to undertake and execute vast plans, possesses none the less an astonishing sagacity and accuracy of observation in petty details. One valet, entrusted with the purveyance, had obtained permission to wear the cassock. "Unless he be much changed in his humour," writes Mgr. de Laval, "it would be well to send him back to France; and I may even opine that, whatever change might appear in him, he would be unfitted to administer a living, the basis of his character being very rustic, gross, and displeasing, and unsuitable for ecclesiastical functions, in which one is constantly obliged to converse and deal with one's neighbours, both children and adults. Having given him the cassock and having admitted him to the refectory, I hardly see any other means of getting rid of him than to send him back to France."

In his correspondence with Saint-Vallier, Laval gives an account of the various steps which he was taking at court to maintain the integrity of the diocese of Quebec. This was, for a short time, at stake. The Récollets, who had followed La Salle in his expeditions, were trying with some chance of success to have the valley of the Mississippi and Louisiana made an apostolic vicariate independent of Canada. Laval finally gained his cause; the jurisdiction of the bishopric of Quebec over all the countries of North America which belonged to France was maintained, and later the Seminary of Quebec sent missionaries to Louisiana and to the Mississippi.

But the most important questions, which formed the principal subject both of his preoccupations and of his letters, are that of the establishment of the Récollets in the Upper Town of Quebec, that of a plan for a permanent mission at Baie St. Paul, and above all, that of the tithes and the support of the priests. This last question brought about between him and Mgr. de Saint-Vallier a most complete conflict of views. Yet the differences of opinion between the two servants of God never prevented them from esteeming each other highly. The following letter does as much honour to him who wrote it as to him to whom such homage is rendered: "The noble house of Laval from which he sprang," writes Mgr. de Saint-Vallier, "the right of primogeniture which he renounced on entering upon the ecclesiastical career; the exemplary life which he led in France before there was any thought of raising him to the episcopacy; the assiduity with which he governed so long the Church in Canada; the constancy and firmness which he showed in surmounting all the obstacles which opposed on divers occasions the rectitude of his intentions and the welfare of his dear flock; the care which he took of the French colony and his efforts for the conversion of the savages; the expeditions which he undertook several times in the interests of both; the zeal which impelled him to return to France to seek a successor; his disinterestedness and the humility which he manifested in offering and in giving so willingly his frank resignation; finally, all the great virtues which I see him practise every day in the seminary where I sojourn with him, would well deserve here a most hearty eulogy, but his modesty imposes silence upon me, and the veneration in which he is held wherever he is known is praise more worthy than I could give him...."

Mgr. de Saint-Vallier left Quebec for France on November 18th, 1686, only a few days after a fire which consumed the Convent of the Ursulines; the poor nuns, who had not been able to snatch anything from the flames, had to accept, until the re-construction of their convent, the generous shelter offered them by the hospitable ladies of the Hôtel-Dieu. Mgr. de Saint-Vallier did not disembark at the port of La Rochelle until forty-five days after his departure, for this voyage was one continuous storm.

[9]A right, belonging formerly to the kings of France, of enjoying the revenues of vacant bishoprics.

CHAPTER XV

MGR. DE LAVAL COMES FOR THE LAST TIME TO CANADA

Mgr. de Saint-Vallier received the most kindly welcome from the king: he availed himself of it to request some aid on behalf of the priests of the seminary whom age and infirmity condemned to retirement. He obtained it, and received, besides, fifteen thousand francs for the building of an episcopal palace. He decided, in fact, to withdraw from the seminary, in order to preserve complete independence in the exercise of his high duties. Laval learned with sorrow of this decision; he, who had always clung to the idea of union with his seminary and of having but one common fund with this house, beheld his successor adopt an opposite line of conduct. Another cause of division rose between the two prelates; the too great generosity of Mgr. de Saint-Vallier had brought the seminary into financial embarrassment. The Marquis de Seignelay, then minister, thought it wiser under such circumstances to postpone till later the return of Mgr. de Laval to Canada. The venerable bishop, whatever it must have cost him, adhered to this decision with a wholly Christian resignation. "You will know by the enclosed letters," he writes to the priests of the Seminary of Quebec, "what compels me to stay in France. I had no sooner received my sentence than our Lord granted me the favour of inspiring me to go before the most Holy Sacrament and make a sacrifice of all my desires and of that which is the dearest to me in the world. I began by making the *amende honorable* to the justice of God, who deigned to extend to me the mercy of recognizing that it was in just punishment of my sins and lack of faith that His providence deprived me of the blessing of returning to a place where I had so greatly offended; and I told Him, I think with a cheerful heart and a spirit of humility, what the high priest Eli said when Samuel declared to him from God what was to happen to him: 'Dominus est: quod bonum est in oculis suis faciat.' But since the will of our Lord does not reject a contrite and humble heart, and since He both abases and exalts, He gave me to know that the greatest favour He could grant me was to give me a share in the trials which He deigned to bear in His life and death for love of us; in thanksgiving for which I said a Te Deum with a heart filled with joy and consolation in my soul: for, as to the lower nature, it is left in the bitterness which it must bear. It is a hurt and a wound which will be difficult to heal and which apparently will last until my death, unless it please Divine Providence, which disposes of men's hearts as it pleases, to bring about some change in the condition of affairs. This will be when it pleases God, and as it may please Him, without His creatures being able to oppose it."

In Canada the return of the revered Mgr. de Laval was impatiently expected, and the governor, M. de Denonville, himself wrote that "in the present state of public affairs it was necessary that the former bishop should return, in order to influence men's minds, over which he had a great ascendency by reason of his character and his reputation for sanctity." Some persons wrongfully attributed to the influence of Saint-Vallier the order which detained the worthy bishop in France; on the contrary, Saint-Vallier had said one day to the minister, "It would be very hard for a bishop who has founded this church and who desires to go and die in its midst, to see himself detained in France. If Mgr. de Laval should stay here the blame would be cast upon his successor, against whom for this reason many people would be ill disposed."

M. de Denonville desired the more eagerly the return of this prelate so beloved in New France, since difficulties were arising on every hand. Convinced that peace with the Iroquois could not last, he began by amassing provisions and ammunition at Fort Cataraqui, without heeding the protests of Colonel Dongan, the most vigilant and most experienced enemy of French domination in America; then he busied himself with fortifying Montreal. He visited the place, appointed as its governor the Chevalier de Callières, a former captain in the regiment of Navarre, and in the spring of 1687 employed six hundred men under the direction of M. du Luth, royal engineer, in the erection of a palisade. These wooden defences, as was to be expected, were not durable and demanded repairs every year. The year 1686, which had begun with the conquest of the southern portion of Hudson Bay, was spent almost entirely in preparations for war and negotiations for peace; the Iroquois, nevertheless, continued their inroads. Finally M. de Denonville, having received during the following spring eight hundred poor recruits under the command of Vaudreuil, was ready for his expedition. Part of these reinforcements were at once sent to Montreal, where M. de Callières was gathering a body of troops on St. Helen's Island: eight hundred and thirty-two regulars, one thousand Canadians, and three hundred Indian allies, all burning with the desire of distinguishing themselves, awaited now only the signal for departure.

"With this superiority of forces," says one author, "Denonville conceived, however, the unfortunate idea of beginning hostilities by an act which dishonoured the French name among the savages, that name which, in spite of their great irritation, they had always feared and respected." With the purpose of striking terror into the Iroquois he caused to be seized the chiefs whom the Five Nations had sent as delegates to Cataraqui at the request of Father de Lamberville, and sent them to France to serve on board the royal galleys. This violation of the law of nations aroused the fury of the Iroquois, and two missionaries, Father Lamberville and Millet, though entirely innocent of this crime, escaped torture only with difficulty. The king disapproved wholly of this treason, and returned the prisoners to Canada; others who, at Fort Frontenac, had been taken by M. de Champigny in as treacherous a manner, were likewise restored to liberty.

The army, divided into four bodies, set out on June 11th, 1687, in four hundred boats. It was joined at Sand River, on the shore of Lake Ontario, by six hundred men from Detroit, and advanced inland. After having passed through two very dangerous defiles, the French were suddenly attacked by eight hundred of the enemy ambushed in the bed of a stream. At first surprised, they promptly recovered from their confusion, and put the savages to flight. Some sixty Iroquois were wounded in this encounter, and forty-five whom they left dead on the field of battle were eaten by the Ottawas, according to the horrible custom of these cannibals. They entered then into the territory of the Tsonnontouans, which was found deserted; everything had been reduced to ashes, except an immense quantity of maize, to which they set fire; they killed also a prodigious number of swine, but they did not meet with a single Indian.

Instead of pursuing the execution of these reprisals by marching against the other nations, M. de Denonville proceeded to Niagara, where he built a fort. The garrison of a hundred men which he left there succumbed in its entirety to a mysterious epidemic, probably caused by the poor quality of the provisions. Thus the campaign did not produce results proportionate to the preparations which had been made; it humbled the Iroquois, but by this very fact it excited their rage and desire for vengeance; so true is it that half-measures are more dangerous than complete inaction. They were, besides, cleverly goaded on by Governor Dongan. Towards the end of the summer they ravaged the whole western part of the colony, and carried their audacity to the point of burning houses and killing several persons on the Island of Montreal.

M. de Denonville understood that he could not carry out a second expedition; disease had caused great havoc among the population and the soldiers, and he could no longer count on the Hurons of Michilimackinac, who kept up secret relations with the Iroquois. He was willing to conclude peace, and consented to demolish Fort Niagara and to bring back the Iroquois chiefs who had been sent to France to row in the galleys. The conditions were already accepted on both sides, when the negotiations were suddenly interrupted by the duplicity of Kondiaronk, surnamed the Rat, chief of the Michilimackinac Hurons. This man, the most cunning and crafty of Indians, a race which has nothing tolearn in point of astuteness from the shrewdest diplomat, had offered his services against the Iroquois to the governor, who had accepted them. Enkindled with the desire of distinguishing himself by some brilliant deed, he arrives with a troop of Hurons at Fort

Frontenac, where he learns that a treaty is about to be concluded between the French and the Iroquois. Enraged at not having even been consulted in this matter, fearing to see the interests of his nation sacrificed, he lies in wait with his troop at Famine Creek, falls upon the delegates, and, killing a number of them, makes the rest prisoners. On the statement of the latter that they were going on an embassy to Ville-Marie, he feigns surprise, and is astonished that the French governor-general should have sent him to attack men who were going to treat with him. He then sets them at liberty, keeping a single one of them, whom he hastens to deliver to M. de Durantaye, governor of Michilimackinac; the latter, ignorant of the negotiations with the Iroquois, has the prisoner shot in spite of the protestations of the wretched man, who the Rat pretends is mad. The plan of the Huron chief has succeeded; it remains now only to reap the fruits of it. He frees an old Iroquois who has long been detained in captivity and sends him to announce to his compatriots that the French are seeking in the negotiations a cowardly means of ridding themselves of their foes. This news exasperated the Five Nations; henceforth peace was impossible, and the Iroquois went to join the English, with whom, on the pretext of the dethronement of James II, war was again about to break out. M. de Callières, governor of Montreal, set out for France to lay before the king a plan for the conquest of New York; the monarch adopted it, but, not daring to trust its execution to M. de Denonville, he recalled him in order to entrust it to Count de Frontenac, now again appointed governor.

We can easily conceive that in the danger thus threatening the colony M. de Denonville should have taken pains to surround himself with all the men whose aid might be valuable to him. "You will have this year," wrote M. de Brisacier to M. Glandelet, "the joy of seeing again our two prelates. You will find the first more holy and more than ever dead to himself; and the second will appear to you all that you can desire him to be for the particular consolation of the seminary and the good of New France." On the request of the governor-general, in fact, Mgr. de Laval saw the obstacle disappear which had opposed his departure, and he hastened to take advantage of it. He set out in the spring of 1688, at that period of the year when vegetation begins to display on all sides its festoons of verdure and flowers, and transforms Normandy and Touraine, that garden of France, into genuine groves; the calm of the air, the perfumed breezes of the south, the arrival of the southern birds with their rich and varied plumage, all contribute to make these days the fairest and sweetest of the year; but, in his desire to reach as soon as possible the country where his presence was deemed necessary, the venerable prelate did not wait for the spring sun to dry the roads soaked by the rains of winter; accordingly, in spite of his infirmities, he was obliged to travel to La Rochelle on horseback. However, he could not embark on the ship *Le Soleil d'Afrique* until about the middle of April.

His duties as Bishop of Quebec had ended on January 25th preceding, the day of the episcopal consecration of M. de Saint-Vallier. It would seem that Providence desired that the priestly career of the prelate and his last co-workers should end at the same time. Three priests of the Seminary of Quebec went to receive in heaven almost at the same period the reward of their apostolic labours. M. Thomas Morel died on September 23rd, 1687; M. Jean

Guyon on January 10th, 1688; and M. Dudouyt on the fifteenth of the same month. This last loss, especially, caused deep grief to Mgr. de Laval. He desired that the heart of the devoted missionary should rest in that soil of New France for which it had always beat, and he brought it with him. The ceremony of the burial at Quebec of the heart of M. Dudouyt was extremely touching; the whole population was present. Up to his latest day this priest had taken the greatest interest in Canada, and the letter which he wrote to the seminary a few days before his death breathes the most ardent charity; it particularly enjoined upon all patience and submission to authority.

The last official document signed by Mgr. de Laval as titulary bishop was an addition to the statutes and rules which he had previously drawn up for the Chapter of the city of Champlain. He wrote at the same time: "It remains for me now, sirs and dearly beloved brethren, only to thank you for the good affection that you preserve towards me, and to assure you that it will not be my fault if I do not go at the earliest moment to rejoin you in the growing Church which I have ever cherished as the portion and heritage which it has pleased our Lord to preserve for me during nearly thirty years. I supplicate His infinite goodness that he into whose hands He has caused it to pass by my resignation may repair all my faults."

The prelate landed on June 3rd. "The whole population," says the Abbé Ferland, "was heartened and rejoiced by the return of Mgr. de Laval, who came back to Canada to end his days among his former flock. His virtues, his long and arduous labours in New France, his sincere love for the children of the country, had endeared him to the Canadians; they felt their trust in Providence renewed on beholding again him who, with them, at their head, had passed through many years of trial and suffering." He hardly took time to rest, but set out at once for Montreal, where he was anxious to deliver in person to the Sulpicians the document of spiritual and devotional union which had been quite recently signed at Paris by the Seminary of St. Sulpice and by that of the Foreign Missions. Returning to Quebec, he had the pleasure of receiving his successor on the arrival of the latter, who disembarked on July 31st, 1688.

The reception of Mgr. de Saint-Vallier was as cordial as that offered two months before to his predecessor. "As early as four o'clock in the morning," we read in the annals of the Ursulines, "the whole population was alert to hasten preparations. Some arranged the avenue along which the new bishop was to pass, others raised here and there the standard of the lilies of France. In the course of the morning Mgr. de Laval, accompanied by several priests, betook himself to the vessel to salute his successor whom the laws of the old French etiquette kept on board his ship until he had replied to all the compliments prepared for him. Finally, about two o'clock in the afternoon, the whole clergy, the civil and military authorities, and the people having assembled on the quay, Mgr. de Saint-Vallier made his appearance, addressed first by M. de Bernières in the name of the clergy. He was next greeted by the mayor, in the name of the whole town, then the procession began to move, with military music at its head, and the new bishop was conducted to the cathedral between two files of musketeers, who did not fail to salute him and to fire volleys along the route." "The thanksgiving hymn which re-echoed under the vaults of the holy temple found an echo in all hearts," we read in another account; "and the least happy was not that of the worthy prelate who thus inaugurated his long and laborious episcopal career."

CHAPTER XVI

MASSACRE OF LACHINE

The virtue of Mgr. de Laval lacked the supreme consecration of misfortune. A wearied but triumphant soldier, the venerable shepherd of souls, coming back to dwell in the bishopric of Quebec, the witness of his first apostolic labours, gave himself into the hands of his Master to disappear and die. "Lord," he said with Simeon, "now lettest thou thy servant depart in peace according to thy word." But many griefs still remained to test his resignation to the Divine Will, and the most shocking disaster mentioned in our annals was to sadden his last days. The year 1688 had passed peacefully enough for the colony, but it was only the calm which is the forerunner of the storm. The Five Nations employed their time in secret organization; the French, lulled in this deceptive security, particularly by news which had come from M. de Valrennes, in command of Fort Frontenac, to whom the Iroquois had declared that they were coming down to Montreal to make peace, had left the forts to return to their dwellings and to busy themselves with the work of the fields. Moreover, the Chevalier de Vaudreuil, who commanded at Montreal in the absence of M. deCallières, who had gone to France, carried his lack of foresight to the extent of permitting the officers stationed in the country to leave their posts. It is astonishing to note such imprudent neglect on the part of men who must have known the savage nature. Rancour is the most deeply-rooted defect in the Indian, and it was madness to think that the Iroquois could have forgotten so soon the insult inflicted on their arms by the expedition of M. de Denonville, or the breach made in their independence by the abduction of their chiefs sent to France as convicts. The warning of their approaching incursion had meanwhile reached Quebec through a savage named Ataviata; unfortunately, the Jesuit Fathers had no confidence in this Indian; they assured the governor-general that Ataviata was a worthless fellow, and M. de Denonville made the mistake of listening too readily to these prejudices and of not at least redoubling his precautions.

It was on the night between August 4th and 5th, 1689; all was quiet on the Island of Montreal. At the end of the evening's conversation, that necessary complement of every well-filled day, the men had hung their pipes, the faithful comrades of their labour, to a rafter of the ceiling; the women had put away their knitting or pushed aside in a corner their indefatigable spinning-wheel, and all had hastened to seek in sleep new strength for the labour of the morrow. Outside, the elements were unchained, the rain and hail were raging. As daring as the Normans when they braved on frail vessels the fury of the seas, the Iroquois, to the number of fifteen hundred, profited by the storm to traverse Lake St. Louis in their bark canoes, and landed silently on the shore at Lachine. They took care not to approach the forts; the darkness was so thick that the soldiers discovered nothing unusual and did not fire the cannon as was the custom on the approach of the enemy. Long before daybreak the savages, divided into a number of squads, had surrounded the houses within a radius of several miles. Suddenly a piercing signal is given by the chiefs, and at once a horrible clamour rends the air; the terrifying war-cry of the

Iroquois has roused the sleepers and raised the hair on the heads of the bravest. The colonists leap from their couches, but they have no time to seize their weapons; demons who seem to be vomited forth by hell have already broken in the doors and windows. The dwellings which the Iroquois cannot penetrate are delivered over to the flames, but the unhappy ones who issue from them in confusion to escape the tortures of the fire are about to be abandoned to still more horrible torments. The pen refuses to describe the horrors of this night, and the imagination of Dante can hardly in his "Inferno" give us an idea of it. The butchers killed the cattle, burned the houses, impaled women, compelled fathers to cast their children into the flames, spitted other little ones still alive and compelled their mothers to roast them. Everything was burned and pillaged except the forts, which were not attacked; two hundred persons of all ages and of both sexes perished under torture, and about fifty, carried away to the villages, were bound to the stake and burned by a slow fire. Nevertheless the great majority of the inhabitants were able to escape, thanks to the strong liquors kept in some of the houses, with which the savages made ample acquaintance. Some of the colonists took refuge in the forts, others were pursued into the woods.

Meanwhile the alarm had spread in Ville-Marie. M. de Denonville, who was there, gives to the Chevalier de Vaudreuil the order to occupy Fort Roland with his troops and a hundred volunteers. De Vaudreuil hastens thither, accompanied by de Subercase and other officers; they are all eager to measure their strength with the enemy, but the order of Denonville is strict, they must remain on the defensive and run no risk. By dint of insistence, Subercase obtained permission to make a sortie with a hundred volunteers; at the moment when he was about to set out he had to yield the command to M. de Saint-Jean, who was higher in rank. The little troop went and entrenched itself among the débris of a burned house and exchanged an ineffectual fire with the savages ambushed in a clump of trees. They soon perceived a party of French and friendly Indians who, coming from Fort Rémy, were proceeding towards them in great danger of being surrounded by the Iroquois, who were already sobered. The volunteers wished to rush out to meet this reinforcement, but their commander, adhering to his instructions, which forbade him to push on farther, restrained them. What might have been foreseen happened: the detachment from Fort Rémy was exterminated. Five of its officers were taken and carried off towards the Iroquois villages, but succeeded in escaping on the way, except M. de la Rabeyre, who was bound to the stake and perished in torture.

On reading these details one cannot understand the inactivity of the French: it would seem that the authorities had lost their heads. We cannot otherwise explain the lack of foresight of the officers absent from their posts, the pusillanimous orders of the governor to M. de Vaudreuil, his imprudence in sending too weak a troop through the dangerous places, the lack of initiative on the part of M. de Saint-Jean, finally, the absolute lack of energy and audacity, the complete absence of that ardour which is inherent in the French character.

After this disaster the troops returned to the forts, and the surrounding district, abandoned thus to the fury of the barbarians, was ravaged in all directions. The Iroquois, proud of the terror which they inspired, threatened the city itself; we note by the records of Montreal that on August 25th there were buried two soldiers killed by the savages, and that on September 7th following, Jean Beaudry suffered the same fate. Finding nothing more to pillage or to burn, they passed to the opposite shore, and plundered the village of Lachesnaie. They massacred a portion of the population, which was composed of seventy-two persons, and carried off the rest. They did not withdraw until the autumn, dragging after them two hundred captives, including fifty prisoners taken at Lachine.

This terrible event, which had taken place at no great distance from them, and the news of which re-echoed in their midst, struck the inhabitants of Quebec with grief and terror. Mgr. de Laval was cruelly affected by it, but, accustomed to adore in everything the designs of God, he seized the occasion to invoke Him with more fervour; he immediately ordered in his seminary public prayers to implore the mercy of the Most High. M. de Frontenac, who was about to begin his second administration, learned the sinister news on his arrival at Quebec on October 15th. He set out immediately for Montreal, which he reached on the twenty-seventh of the same month. He visited the environments, and found only ruins and ashes where formerly rose luxurious dwellings.

War had just been rekindled between France and Great Britain. The governor had not men enough for vast operations, accordingly he prepared to organize a guerilla warfare. While the Abenaquis, those faithful allies, destroyed the settlements of the English in Acadia and killed nearly two hundred persons there,

Count de Frontenac sent in the winter of 1689-90, three detachments against New England; all three were composed of only a handful of men, but these warriors were well seasoned. In the rigorous cold of winter, traversing innumerable miles on their snowshoes, sinking sometimes into the icy water, sleeping in the snow, carrying their supplies on their backs, they surprised the forts which they went to attack, where one would never have believed that men could execute so rash an enterprise. Thus the three detachments were alike successful, and the forts of Corlaer in the state of New York, of Salmon Falls in New Hampshire, and of Casco on the seaboard, were razed.

The English avenged these reverses by capturing Port Royal. Encouraged by this success, they sent Phipps at the head of a large troop to seize Quebec, while Winthrop attacked Montreal with three thousand men, a large number of whom were Indians. Frontenac hastened to Quebec with M. de Callières, governor of Montreal, the militia and the regular troops. Already the fortifications had been protected against surprise by new and well-arranged entrenchments. The hostile fleet appeared on October 16th, 1690, and Phipps sent an officer to summon the governor to surrender the place. The envoy, drawing out his watch, declared with arrogance to the Count de Frontenac that he would give him an hour to decide. "I will answer you by the mouth of my cannon," replied the representative of Louis XIV. The cannon replied so well that at the first shot the admiral's flag fell into the water; the Canadians, braving the balls and bullets which rained about them, swam out to get it, and this trophy remained hanging in the cathedral of Quebec until the conquest. The *Histoire de l'Hôtel-*

Dieu de Québec depicts for us very simply the courage and piety of the inhabitants during this siege. "The most admirable thing, and one which surely drew the blessing of Heaven upon Quebec was that during the whole siege no public devotion was interrupted. The city is arranged so that the roads which lead to the churches are seen from the harbour; thus several times a day were beheld processions of men and women going to answer the summons of the bells. The English noticed them; they called M. de Grandeville (a brave Canadian, and clerk of the farm of Tadousac, whom they had made prisoner) and asked him what it was. He answered them simply: 'It is mass, vespers, and the benediction.' By this assurance the citizens of Quebec disconcerted them; they were astonished that women dared to go out; they judged by this that we were very easy in our minds, though this was far from being the case."

It is not surprising that the colonists should have fought valiantly when their bishops and clergy set the example of devotion, when the Jesuits remained constantly among the defenders to encourage and assist on occasion the militia and the soldiers, when Mgr. de Laval, though withdrawn from the conduct of religious affairs, without even the right of sitting in the Sovereign Council, animated the population by his patriotic exhortations. To prove to the inhabitants that the cause which they defended by struggling for their homes was just and holy, at the same time as to place the cathedral under the protection of Heaven, he suggested the idea of hanging on the spire of the cathedral a picture of the Holy Family. This picture was not touched by the balls and bullets, and was restored after the siege to the Ursulines, to whom it belonged.

All the attempts of the English failed; in a fierce combat at Beauport they were repulsed. There perished the brave Le Moyne de Sainte-Hélène; there, too, forty pupils of the seminary established at St. Joachim by Mgr. de Laval distinguished themselves by their bravery and contributed to the victory. Already Phipps had lost six hundred men. He decided to retreat. To cap the climax of misfortune, his fleet met in the lower part of the river with a horrible storm; several of his ships were driven by the winds as far as the Antilles, and the rest arrived only with great difficulty at Boston. Winthrop's army, disorganized by disease and discord, had already scattered.

A famine which followed the siege tried the whole colony, and Laval had to suffer by it as well as the seminary, for neither had hesitated before the sacrifices necessary for the general weal. "All the furs and furniture of the Lower Town were in the seminary," wrote the prelate; "a number of families had taken refuge there, even that of the intendant. This house could not refuse in such need all the sacrifices of charity which were possible, at the expense of a great portion of the provisions which were kept there. The soldiers and others have taken and consumed at least one hundred cords of wood and more than fifteen hundred planks. In brief, in cattle and other damages the loss to the seminary will amount to a round thousand crowns. But we must on occasions of this sort be patient, and do all the good we can without regard to future need."

The English were about to suffer still other reverses. In 1691 Major Schuyler, with a small army composed in part of savages, came and surprised below the fort of the Prairie de la Madeleine a camp of between seven and eight hundred soldiers, whose leader, M. de Saint-Cirque, was slain; but the French, recovering, forced the major to retreat, and M. de Valrennes, who hastened up from Chambly with a body of inhabitants and Indians, put the enemy to flight after a fierce struggle. The English failed also in Newfoundland; they were unable to carry Fort Plaisance, which was defended by M. de Brouillan; but he who was to do them most harm was the famous Pierre Le Moyne d'Iberville, son of Charles Le Moyne. Born in Montreal in 1661, he subsequently entered the French navy. In the year 1696 he was ordered to drive the enemy out of Newfoundland; he seized the capital, St. John's, which he burned, and, marvellous to relate, with only a hundred and twenty-five men he subdued the whole island, slew nearly two hundred of the English, and took six or seven hundred prisoners. The following year he set out with five ships to take possession of Hudson Bay. One day his vessel found itself alone before Fort Nelson, facing three large ships of the enemy; to the amazement of the English, instead of surrendering, d'Iberville rushes upon them. In a fierce fight lasting four hours, he sinks the strongest, compels the second to surrender, while the third flees under full sail. Fort Bourbon surrendered almost at once, and Hudson Bay was captured.

After the peace d'Iberville explored the mouths of the Mississippi, erected several forts, founded the city of Mobile, and became the first governor of Louisiana. When the war began again, the king gave him a fleet of sixteen vessels to oppose the English in the Indies. He died of an attack of fever in 1706.

During this time, the Iroquois were as dangerous to the French by their inroads and devastations as the Abenaquis were to the English colonies; accordingly Frontenac wished to subdue them. In the summer of 1696, braving the fatigue and privations so hard to bear for a man of his age, Frontenac set out from Ile Perrot with more than two thousand men, and landed at the mouth of the Oswego River. He found at Onondaga only the smoking remains of the village to which the savages had themselves set fire, and the corpses of two Frenchmen who had died in torture. He marched next against the Oneidas; all had fled at his approach, and he had to be satisfied with laying waste their country. There remained three of the Five Nations to punish, but winter was coming on and Frontenac did not wish to proceed further into the midst of invisible enemies, so he returned to Quebec.

The following year it was learned that the Treaty of Ryswick had just been concluded between France and England. France kept Hudson Bay, but Louis XIV pledged himself to recognize William III as King of England. The Count de Frontenac had not the good fortune of crowning his brilliant career by a treaty with the savages; he died on November 28th, 1698, at the age of seventy-eight years. In reaching this age without exceeding it, he presented a new point of resemblance to his model, Louis the Great, according to whom he always endeavoured to shape his conduct, and who was destined to die at the age of seventy-seven.

[Note.—The incident of the flag mentioned above on page 230 is treated at greater length in Dr. Le Sueur's *Frontenac*, pp. 295-8, in the "Makers of Canada" series. He takes a somewhat different view of the event.—Ed.]

CHAPTER XVII

THE LABOURS OF OLD AGE

The peace lasted only four years. M. de Callières, who succeeded Count de Frontenac, was able, thanks to his prudence and the devotion of the missionaries, to gather at Montreal more than twelve hundred Indian chiefs or warriors, and to conclude peace with almost all the tribes. Chief Kondiaronk had become a faithful friend of the French; it was to his good-will and influence that they were indebted for the friendship of a large number of Indian tribes. He died at Montreal during these peaceful festivities and was buried with pomp.

The war was about to break out anew, in 1701, with Great Britain and the other nations of Europe, because Louis XIV had accepted for his grandson and successor the throne of Spain. M. de Callières died at this juncture; his successor, Philippe de Rigaud, Marquis de Vaudreuil, brought the greatest energy to the support in Canada of a struggle which was to end in the dismemberment of the colony. God permitted Mgr. de Laval to die before the Treaty of Utrecht, whose conditions would have torn the patriotic heart of the venerable prelate.

Other reasons for sorrow he did not lack, especially when Mgr. de Saint-Vallier succeeded, on his visit to the king in 1691, in obtaining a reversal of the policy marked out for the seminary by the first bishop of the colony; this establishment would be in the future only a seminary like any other, and would have no other mission than that of the training of priests. By a decree of the council of February 2nd, 1692, the number of the directors of the seminary was reduced to five, who were to concern themselves principally with the training of young men who might have a vocation for the ecclesiastical life; they might also devote themselves to missions, with the consent of the bishop. No ecclesiastic had the right of becoming an associate of the seminary without the permission of the bishop, within whose province it was to employ the former associates for the service of his diocese with the consent of the superiors. The last part of the decree provided that the four thousand francs given by the king for the diocese of Quebec should be distributed in equal portions, one for the seminary and the two others for the priests and the church buildings. As to the permanence of priests, the decree issued by the king for the whole kingdom was to be adhered to in Canada. In the course of the same year Mgr. de Saint-Vallier obtained, moreover, from the sovereign the authority to open at Quebec in Notre-Dame des Anges, the former convent of the Récollets, a general hospital for the poor, which was entrusted to the nuns of the Hôtel-Dieu. The poor who might be admitted to it would be employed at work proportionate to their strength, and more particularly in the tilling of the farms belonging to the establishment. If we remember that Mgr. de Laval had consecrated twenty years of his life to giving his seminary, by a perfect union between its members and his whole clergy, a formidable power in the colony, a power which in his opinion could be used only for the good of the Church and in the public interest, and that he now saw his efforts annihilated forever, we cannot help admiring the resignation with which he managed to accept this destruction of his dearest work. And not only did he bow before the impenetrable designs of

Providence, but he even used his efforts to pacify those around him whose excitable temperaments might have brought about conflicts with the authorities. The Abbé Gosselin quotes in this connection the following example: "A priest, M. de Francheville, thought he had cause for complaint at the behaviour of his bishop towards him, and wrote him a letter in no measured terms, but he had the good sense to submit it previously to Mgr. de Laval, whom he regarded as his father. The aged bishop expunged from this letter all that might wound Mgr. de Saint-Vallier, and it was sent with the corrections which he desired." The venerable prelate did not content himself with avoiding all that might cause difficulties to his successor; he gave him his whole aid in any circumstances, and in particular in the foundation of a convent of Ursulines at Three Rivers, and when the general hospital was threatened in its very existence. "Was it not a spectacle worthy of the admiration of men and angels," exclaims the Abbé Fornel in his funeral oration on Mgr. de Saint-Vallier, "to see the first Bishop of Quebec and his successor vieing one with the other in a noble rivalry and in a struggle of religious fervour for the victory in exercises of piety? Have they not both been seen harmonizing and reconciling together the duties of seminarists and canons; of canons by their assiduity in the recitation of the breviary, and of seminarists in condescending to the lowest duties, such as sweeping and serving in the kitchen?" The patience and trust in God of Mgr. de Laval were rewarded by the following letter which he received from Father La Chaise, confessor to King Louis XIV: "I have received with much respect and gratitude two letters with which you have honoured me. I have blessed God that He has preserved you for His glory and the good of the Church in Canada in a period of deadly mortality;

and I pray every day that He may preserve you some years more for His service and the consolation of your old friends and servants. I hope that you will maintain towards them to the end your good favour and interest, and that those who would wish to make them lose these may be unable to alter them. You will easily judge how greatly I desire that our Fathers may merit the continuation of your kindness, and may preserve a perfect union with the priests of your seminary, by the sacrifice which I desire they should make to the latter, in consideration of you, of the post of Tamarois, in spite of all the reasons and the facility for preserving it to them...."

The mortality to which the reverend father alludes was the result of an epidemic which carried off, in 1700, a great number of persons. Old men in particular were stricken, and M. de Bernières among others fell a victim to the scourge. It is very probable that this affliction was nothing less than the notorious influenza which, in these later years, has cut down so many valuable lives throughout the world. The following years were still more terrible for the town; smallpox carried off one-fourth of the population of Quebec. If we add to these trials the disaster of the two conflagrations which consumed the seminary, we shall have the measure of the troubles which at this period overwhelmed the city of Champlain. The seminary, begun in 1678, had just been barely completed. It was a vast edifice of stone, of grandiose appearance; a sun dial was set above a majestic door of two leaves, the approach to which was a fine stairway of cut stone. "The building," wrote Frontenac in 1679, "is very large and has four storeys, the walls are seven feet thick, the cellars and pantries are vaulted, the lower windows have embrasures, and the roof is of slate brought from France." On November 15th, 1701, the priests of the seminary had taken their pupils to St. Michel, near Sillery, to a country house which belonged to them. About one in the afternoon fire broke out in the seminary buildings. The inhabitants hastened up from all directions to the spot and attempted with the greatest energy to stay the progress of the flames. Idle efforts! The larger and the smaller seminary, the priests' house, the chapel barely completed, were all consumed, with the exception of some furniture and a little plate and tapestry. The cathedral was saved, thanks to the efforts of the state engineer, M. Levasseur de Néré, who succeeded in cutting off the communication of the sacred temple with the buildings in flames. Mgr. de Laval, confined then to a bed of pain, avoided death by escaping half-clad; he accepted for a few days, together with the priests of the seminary, the generous hospitality offered them by the Jesuit Fathers. In order not to be too long a burden to their hosts, they caused to be prepared for their lodgment the episcopal palace which had been begun by Mgr. de Saint-Vallier. They removed there on December 4th following. The scholars had been divided between the episcopal palace and the house of the Jesuits. "The prelate," says Sister Juchereau, "bore this affliction with perfect submission to the will of God, without uttering any complaint. It must have been, however, the more grievous to him since it was he who had planned and erected the seminary, since he was its father and founder, and since he saw ruined in one day the fruit of his labour of many years." Thanks to the generosity of the king, who granted aid to the extent of four thousand francs, it was possible to begin rebuilding at once. But the trials of the priests were not yet over. "On the first day of

October, 1705," relate the annals of the Ursulines, "the priests of the seminary were afflicted by a second fire through the fault of a carpenter who was preparing some boards in one end of the new building. While smoking he let fall in a room full of shavings some sparks from his pipe. The fire being kindled, it consumed in less than an hour all the upper storeys. Only those which were vaulted were preserved. The priests estimate that they have lost more in this second fire than in the first. They are lodged below, waiting till Providence furnishes them with the means to restore their building. The Jesuit Fathers have acted this time with the same charity and cordiality as on the former occasion. Mgr. L'Ancien[10] and M. Petit have lived nearly two months in their infirmary. This rest has been very profitable to Monseigneur, for he has come forth from it quite rejuvenated. May the Lord grant that he be preserved a long time yet for the glory of God and the good of Canada!"

When Nehemiah returned to Jerusalem to raise it from its ruins, a great grief seized upon him at the sight of the roofs destroyed, the broken doors, the shattered ramparts of the city of David. In the middle of the night he made the circuit of these ruins, and on the morrow he sought the magistrates and said to them: "You see the distress that we are in? Come, and let us build up the wall of Jerusalem." The same feelings no doubt oppressed the soul of the octogenarian prelate when he saw the walls cracked and blackened, the heaps of ruins, sole remnants of his beloved house. But like Nehemiah he had the support of a great King, and the confidence of succeeding. He set to work at once, and found in the generosity of his flock the means to raise the seminary from its ruins. While he found provisional lodgings for his seminarists, he himself took up quarters in a part of the seminary which had been spared by the flames; he arranged, adjoining his room, a little oratory where he kept the Holy Sacrament, and celebrated mass. There he passed his last days and gave up his fair soul to God.

Mgr. de Saint-Vallier had not like his predecessor the sorrow of seeing fire consume his seminary; he had set out in 1700 for France, and the differences which existed between the two prelates led the monarch to retain Mgr. de Saint-Vallier near him. In 1705 the Bishop of Quebec obtained permission to return to his diocese. But for three years hostilities had already existed between France and England. The bishop embarked with several monks on the *Seine*, a vessel of the Royal Navy. This ship carried a rich cargo valued at nearly a million francs, and was to escort several merchant ships to their destination at Quebec. The convoy fell in, on July 26th, with an English fleet which gave chase to it; the merchant ships fled at full sail, abandoning the *Seine* to its fate. The commander, M. de Meaupou, displayed the greatest valour, but his vessel, having a leeward position, was at a disadvantage; besides, he had committed the imprudence of so loading the deck with merchandise that several cannon could not be used. In spite of her heroic defence, the *Seine* was captured by boarding, the commander and the officers were taken prisoners, and Mgr. de Saint-Vallier remained in captivity in England till 1710.

The purpose of Mgr. de Saint-Vallier's journey to Europe in 1700 had been his desire to have ratified at Rome by the Holy See the canonical union of his abbeys, and the union of the parish of Quebec with the seminary. On setting out he had entrusted the administration of the diocese to MM. Maizerets and Glandelet; as to ordinations, to the administration of the sacrament of confirmation, and to the consecration of the holy oils, Mgr. de Laval would be always there, ready to lavish his zeal and the treasures of his charity. This long absence of the chief of the diocese could not but impose new labours on Mgr. de Laval. Never did he refuse a sacrifice or a duty, and he saw in this an opportunity to increase the sum of good which he intended soon to lay at the foot of the throne of the Most High. He was seventy-nine years of age when, in spite of the havoc then wrought by the smallpox throughout the country, he went as far as Montreal, there to administer the sacrament of confirmation. Two years before his death, he officiated pontifically on Easter Day in the cathedral of Quebec. "On the festival of Sainte Magdalene," say the annals of the general hospital, "we have had the consolation of seeing Mgr. de Laval officiate pontifically morning and evening.... He was accompanied by numerous clergy both from the seminary and from neighbouring missions.... We regarded this favour as a mark of the affection cherished by this holy prelate for our establishment, for he was never wont to officiate outside the cathedral, and even there but rarely on account of his great age. He was then more than eighty years old. The presence of a person so venerable by reason of his character, his virtues, and his great age much enhanced this festival. He gave the nuns a special proof of his good-will in the visit which he deigned to make them in the common hall." The predilection which the pious pontiff constantly preserved for the work of the seminary no whit lessened the protection which he generously granted to all the projects of education in the colony; the daughters of Mother Mary of the Incarnation as well as the assistants of Mother Marguerite Bourgeoys had claims upon his affection. He fostered with all his power the establishment of the Sisters of the Congregation, both at Three Rivers and at Quebec. His numerous works left him but little respite, and this he spent at his school of St. Joachim in the refreshment of quiet and rest. Like all holy men he loved youth, and took pleasure in teaching and directing it. Accordingly, during these years when, in spite of the sixteen *lustra* which had passed over his venerable head, he had to take upon himself during the long absence of his successor the interim duties of the diocese, at least as far as the exclusively episcopal functions were concerned, he learned to understand and appreciate at their true value the sacrifices of the Charron Brothers, whose work was unfortunately to remain fruitless.

In 1688 three pious laymen, MM. Jean François Charron, Pierre Le Ber, and Jean Fredin had established in Montreal a house with a double purpose of charity: to care for the poor and the sick, and to train men and send them to open schools in the country districts. Their plan was approved by the king, sanctioned by the bishop of the diocese, encouraged by the seigneurs of the island, and welcomed by all the citizens with gratitude. In spite of these symptoms of future prosperity the work languished, and the members of the community were separated and scattered one after the other. M. Charron did not lose courage. In 1692 he devoted his large fortune to the foundation of a hospital and a school, and received numerous gifts from charitable persons. Six hospitallers of the order of St. Joseph of the Cross, commonly called Frères Charron, took the gown in 1701, and pronounced their vows in

1704, but the following year they ceased to receive novices. The minister, M. de Pontchartrain, thought "the care of the sick is a task better adapted to women than to men, notwithstanding the spirit of charity which may animate the latter," and he forbade the wearing of the costume adopted by the hospitallers. François Charron, seeing his work nullified, yielded to the inevitable, and confined himself to the training of teachers for country parishes. The existence of this establishment, abandoned by the mother country to its own strength, was to become more and more precarious and feeble. Almost all the hospitallers left the institution to re-enter the world; the care of the sick was entrusted to the Sisters. François Charron made a journey to France in order to obtain the union for the purposes of the hospital of the Brothers of St. Joseph with the Society of St. Sulpice, but he failed in his efforts. He obtained, nevertheless, from the regent an annual subvention of three thousand francs for the training of school-masters (1718). He busied himself at once with finding fitting recruits, and collected eight. The elder sister of our excellent normal schools of the present day seemed then established on solid foundations, but it was not to be so. Brother Charron died on the return voyage, and his institution, though seconded by the Seminary of St. Sulpice, after establishing Brothers in several villages in the environs of Montreal, received from the court a blow from which it did not recover: the regent forbade the masters to assume a uniform dress and to pledge themselves by simple vows. The number of the hospitallers decreased from year to year, and in 1731 the royal government withdrew from them the annual subvention which supported them, however poorly. Finally their institution, after vainly attempting to unite with the Brothers of the Christian Doctrine, ceased to exist in 1745.

Mgr. de Laval so greatly admired the devotion of these worthy men that he exclaimed one day: "Let me die in the house of these Brothers; it is a work plainly inspired by God. I shall die content if only in dying I may contribute something to the shaping or maintenance of this establishment." Again he wrote: "The good M. Charron gave us last year one of their Brothers, who rendered great service to the Mississippi Mission, and he has furnished us another this year. These acquisitions will spare the missionaries much labour.... I beg you to show full gratitude to this worthy servant of God, who is as affectionately inclined to the missions and missionaries as if he belonged to our body. We have even the plan, as well as he, of forming later a community of their Brothers to aid the missions and accompany the missionaries on their journeys. He goes to France and as far as Paris to find and bring back with him some good recruits to aid him in forming a community. Render him all the services you can, as if it were to missionaries themselves. He is a true servant of God." Such testimony is the fairest title to glory for an institution.

[10] A respectfully familiar sobriquet given to Mgr. de Laval.

CHAPTER XVIII

LAST YEARS OF MGR. DE LAVAL

Illness had obliged Mgr. de Laval to hand in his resignation. He wrote, in fact, at this period of his life to M. de Denonville: "I have been for the last two years subject to attacks of vertigo accompanied by heart troubles which are very frequent and increase markedly. I have had one quite recently, on the Monday of the Passion, which seized me at three o'clock in the morning, and I could not raise my head from my bed." His infirmities, which he bore to the end with admirable resignation, especially affected his limbs, which he was obliged to bandage tightly every morning, and which could scarcely bear the weight of his body. To disperse the unwholesome humours, his arm had been cauterized; to cut, carve and hack the poor flesh of humanity formed, as we know, the basis of the scientific and medical equipment of the period. These sufferings, which he brought as a sacrifice to our Divine Master, were not sufficient for him; he continued in spite of them to wear upon his body a coarse hair shirt. He had to serve him only one of those Brothers who devoted their labour to the seminary in exchange for their living and a place at table. This modest servant, named Houssart, had replaced a certain Lemaire, of whom the prelate draws a very interesting portrait in one of his letters: "We must economize," he wrote to the priests of the seminary, "and have only watchful and industrious domestics. We must look after them, else they deteriorate in the seminary. You have the example of the baker, Louis Lemaire, an idler, a gossip, a tattler, a man who, instead of walking behind the coach, would not go unless Monseigneur paid for a carriage for him to follow him to La Rochelle, and lent him his dressing-gown to protect him from the cold. Formerly he worked well at heavy labour at Cap Tourmente; idleness has ruined him in the seminary. As soon as he had reached my room, he behaved like a man worn out, always complaining, coming to help me to bed only when the fancy took him; always extremely vain, thinking he was not dressed according to his position, although he was clad, as you know, more like a nobleman than a peasant, which he was, for I had taken him as a beggar and almost naked at La Rochelle.... As soon as he entered my room he sat down, and rather than be obliged to pretend to see him, I turned my seat so as not to see him.... We should have left that man at heavy work, which had in some sort conquered his folly and pride, and it is possible that he might have been saved. But he has been entirely ruined in the seminary...." This humorous description proves to us well that even in the good old days not all domestics were perfect.

The affectionate and respectful care given by Houssart to his master was such as is not bought with money. Most devoted to the prelate, he has left us a very edifying relation of the life of the venerable bishop, with some touching details. He wrote after his death: "Having had the honour of being continually attached to the service of his Lordship during the last twenty years of his holy life, and his Lordship having had during all that time a great charity towards me and great confidence in my care, you cannot doubt that I contracted a great sympathy, interest and particular attachment for his Lordship." In another letter he speaks to us of the submission of the venerable bishop to the commands of the Church. "He did his best," he writes, "notwithstanding his great age and continual infirmities, to observe all days of abstinence and fasting, both those which are commanded by Holy Church and those which are observed from reasons of devotion in the seminary, and if his Lordship sometimes yielded in this matter to the command of the physicians and the entreaties of the superiors of the seminary, who deemed that he ought not to fast, it was a great mortification for him, and it was only out of especial charity to his dear seminary and the whole of Canada that he yielded somewhat to nature in order not to die so soon...."

Never, in spite of his infirmities, would the prelate fail to be present on Sunday at the cathedral services. When it was impossible for him to go on foot, he had himself carried. His only outings towards the end of his life consisted in his visits to the cathedral or in short walks along the paths of his garden. Whenever his health permitted, he loved to be present at the funerals of those who died in the town; those consolations which he deigned to give to the afflicted families bear witness to the goodness of his heart. "It was something admirable," says Houssart, "to see, firstly, his assiduity in being present at the burial of all who died in Quebec, and his promptness in offering the holy sacrifice of the mass for the repose of their souls, as soon as he had learned of their decease; secondly, his devotion in receiving and preserving the blessed palms, in kissing his crucifix, the image of the Holy Virgin, which he carried always upon him, and placed at nights under his pillow, his badge of servitude and his scapulary which he carried also upon him; thirdly, his respect and veneration for the relics of the saints, the pleasure which he took in reading every day in the Lives of the Saints, and in conversing of their heroic deeds;

fourthly, the holy and constant use which he made of holy water, taking it wherever he might be in the course of the day and every time he awoke in the night, coming very often from his garden to his room expressly to take it, carrying it upon him in a little silver vessel, which he had had made purposely, when he went to the country. His Lordship had so great a desire that every one should take it that he exercised particular care in seeing every day whether the vessels of the church were supplied with it, to fill them when they were empty; and during the winter, for fear that the vessels should freeze too hard and the people could not take any as they entered and left the church, he used to bring them himself every evening and place them by our stove, and take them back at four o'clock in the morning when he went to open the doors."

With a touching humility the pious old man scrupulously conformed to the rules of the seminary and to the orders of the superior of the house. Only a few days before his death, he experienced such pain that Brother Houssart declared his intention of going and asking from the superior of the seminary a dispensation for the sick man from being present at the services. At once the patient became silent; in spite of his tortures not a complaint escaped his lips. It was Holy Wednesday: it was impossible to be absent on that day from religious ceremonies. We do not know which to admire most in such an attitude, whether the piety of the prelate or his submission to the superior of the seminary, since he would have been resigned if he had been forbidden to go to church, or, finally, his energy in stifling the groans which suffering wrenched from his physical nature. Few saints carried mortification and renunciation of terrestrial good as far as he. "He is certainly the mostaustere man in the world and the most indifferent to worldly advantage," wrote Mother Mary of the Incarnation. "He gives away everything and lives like a pauper; and we may truly say that he has the very spirit of poverty. It is not he who will make friends for worldly advancement and to increase his revenue; he is dead to all that.... He practises this poverty in his house, in his living, in his furniture, in his servants, for he has only one gardener, whom he lends to the poor when they need one, and one valet...." This picture falls short of the truth. For forty years he arose at two o'clock in the morning, summer and winter: in his last years illness could only wrest from him one hour more of repose, and he arose then at three o'clock. As soon as he was dressed, he remained at prayer till four and then went to church. He opened the doors himself, and rang the bells for mass, which he said, half an hour later, especially for the poor workmen, who began their day by this pious exercise.

His thanksgiving after the holy sacrifice lasted till seven o'clock, and yet, even in the greatest cold of the severe Canadian winter, he had nothing to warm his frozen limbs but the brazier which he had used to celebrate the mass. A good part of his day, and often of the night, when his sufferings deprived him of sleep, was also devoted to prayer or spiritual reading, and nothing was more edifying than to see the pious octogenarian telling his beads or reciting his breviary while walking slowly through the paths of his garden. He was the first up and the last to retire, and whatever had been his occupations during the day, never did he lie down without having scrupulously observed all the spiritual offices, readings or reciting of beads. It was not, however, that his food gave him a superabundance of physical vigour, for the Trappists did not eat more frugally than he. A soup, which he purposely spoiled by diluting it amply with hot water, a little meat and a crust of very dry bread composed his ordinary fare, and dessert, even on feast days, was absolutely banished from his table. "For his ordinary drink," says Brother Houssart, "he took only hot water slightly flavoured with wine; and every one knows that his Lordship never took either cordial or dainty wines, or any mixture of sweets of any sort whatever, whether to drink or to eat, except that in his last years I succeeded in making him take every evening after his broth, which was his whole supper, a piece of biscuit as large as one's thumb, in a little wine, to aid him to sleep. I may say without exaggeration that his whole life was one continual fast, for he took no breakfast, and every evening only a slight collation.... He used his whole substance in alms and pious works; and when he needed anything, such as clothes, linen, etc., he asked it from the seminary like the humblest of his ecclesiastics. He was most modest in matters of dress, and I had great difficulty in preventing him from wearing his clothes when they were old, dirty and mended. During twenty years he had but two winter cassocks, which he left behind him on his death, the one still quite good, the other all threadbare and mended. To be brief, there was no one in the seminary poorer in dress...." Mgr. de Laval set an example of the principal virtues which distinguish the saints; so he could not fail in that which our Lord incessantly recommends to His disciples, charity! He no longer possessed anything of his own, since he had at the outset abandoned his patrimony to his brother, and since later on he had given to the seminary everything in his possession. But charity makes one ingenious: by depriving himself of what was strictly necessary, could he not yet come to the aid of his brothers in Jesus Christ? "Never was prelate," says his eulogist, M. de la Colombière, "more hostile to grandeur and exaltation.... In scorning grandeur, he triumphed over himself by a poverty worthy of the anchorites of the first centuries, whose rules he faithfully observed to the end of his days. Grace had so thoroughly absorbed in the heart of the prelate the place of the tendencies of our corrupt nature that he seemed to have been born with an aversion to riches, pleasures and honours.... If you have noticed his dress, his furniture and his table, you must be aware that he was a foe to pomp and splendour. There is no village priest in France who is not better nourished, better clad and better lodged than was the Bishop of Quebec. Far from having an equipage suitable to his rank and dignity he had not even a horse of his own. And when, towards the end of his days, his great age and his infirmities did not allow him to walk, if he wished to go out he had to borrow a carriage. Why this economy? In order to have a storehouse full of garments, shoes and blankets, which he distributed gratuitously, with paternal kindness and prudence. This was a business which he never ceased to ply, in which he trusted only to himself, and with which he concerned himself up to his death."

The charity of the prelate was boundless. Not only at the hospital of Quebec did he visit the poor and console them, but he even rendered them services the most repugnant to nature. "He has been seen," says M. de la Colombière, "on a ship where he behaved like St. François-Xavier, where, ministering to the sailors and the passengers, he breathed the bad air and the infection which they exhaled; he has been seen to abandon in their favour all his refreshments, and to give them even his bed, sheets and blankets. To administer the sacraments to them he did not fear to expose his life and the lives of the persons who were most dear to him." When he thus attended the sick who were attacked by contagious fever, he did his duty, even more than his duty; but when he went, without absolute need, and shared in the repugnant cares which the most devoted servants of Christ in the hospitals undertake only after struggles and heroic victory over revolted nature he rose to sublimity. It was because he saw in the poor the suffering members of the Saviour; to love the poor man, it is not enough to wish him well, we must respect him, and we cannot respect him as much as any child of God deserves without seeing in him the image of Jesus Christ himself. No one acquires love for God without being soon wholly enkindled by it; thus it was no longer sufficient for Mgr. de Laval to instruct and console the poor and the sick, he served them also in the most abject duties, going as far as to wash with his own hands their sores and ulcers. A madman, the world will say; why not content one's self with attending those people without indulging in the luxury of heroism so repugnant? This would have sufficed indeed to relieve nature, but would it have taught those incurable and desperate cases that they were the first friends of Jesus Christ, that the Church looked upon them as its jewels, and that their fate from the point of view of eternity was enviable to all? It would have relieved without consoling and raising the poor man to the height which belongs to him in Christian society. Official assistance, with the best intentions in the world, the most ingenious organization and the most perfect working, can, however, never be charity in the perfectly Christian sense of this word. If it could allay all needs and heal all sores it would still have accomplished only half of the task: relieving the body without reaching the soul. And man does not live by bread alone. He who has been disinherited of the boons of fortune, family and health, he who is incurable and who despairs of human joys needs something else besides the most comfortable hospital room that can be imagined; he needs the words which fell from the lips of God: "Blessed are the poor, blessed are they that suffer, blessed are they that mourn." He needs a pitying heart, a tender witness to indigence nobly borne, a respectful friend of his misfortune, still more than that, a worshipper of Jesus hidden in the persons of the poor, the orphan and the sick. They have become rare in the world, these real friends of the poor; the more assistance has become organized, the more charity seems to have lost its true nature; and perhaps we might find in this state of things a radical explanation for those implacable social antagonisms, those covetous desires, those revolts followed by endless repression, which bring about revolutions, and by them all manner of tyranny. Let us first respect the poor, let us love them, let us sincerely admire their condition as one ennobled by God, if we wish them to become reconciled with Him, and reconciled with the world. When the rich man is a Christian, generous and respectful of the poor, when he practises the virtues which most belong to his social position, the poor man is very near to conforming to those virtues which Providence makes his more immediate duty, humility, obedience, resignation to the will of God and trust in Him and in those who rule in His name. The solution of the great social problem lies, as it seems to us, in the spiritual love of the poor. Outside of this, there is only the heathen slave below, and tyranny above with all its terrors. That is what religious enthusiasm foresaw in centuries less well organized but more religious than ours.

CHAPTER XIX

DEATH OF MGR. DE LAVAL

The end of a great career was now approaching. In the summer of 1707, a long and painful illness nearly carried Mgr. de Laval away, but he recovered, and convalescence was followed by manifest improvement. This soul which, like the lamp of the sanctuary, was consumed in the tabernacle of the Most High, revived suddenly at the moment of emitting its last gleams, then suddenly died out in final brilliance. The improvement in the condition of the venerable prelate was ephemeral; the illness which had brought him to the threshold of the tomb proved fatal some weeks later. He died in the midst of his labours, happy in proving by the very origin of the disease which brought about his death, his great love for the Saviour. It was, in fact, in prolonging on Good Friday his pious stations in his chilly church (for our ancestors did not heat their churches, even in seasons of rigorous cold), that he received in his heel the frost-bite of which he died. Such is the name the writers of the time give to this sore; in our days, when science has defined certain maladies formerly misunderstood, it is permissible to suppose that this so-called frost-bite was nothing else than diabetic gangrene. No illusion could be cherished, and the venerable old man, who had not, so to speak, passed a moment of his existence without thinking of death, needed to adapt himself to the idea less than any one else. In order to have nothing more to do than to prepare for his last hour he hastened to settle a question which concerned his seminary: he reduced definitely to eight the number of pensions which he had established in it in 1680. This done, it remained for him now only to suffer and die. The ulcer increased incessantly and the continual pains which he felt became atrocious when it was dressed. His intolerable sufferings drew from him, nevertheless, not cries and complaints, but outpourings of love for God. Like Saint Vincent de Paul, whom the tortures of his last malady could not compel to utter other words than these: "Ah, my Saviour! my good Saviour!" Mgr. de Laval gave vent to these words only: "O, my God! have pity on me! O God of Mercy!" and this cry, the summary of his whole life: "Let Thy holy will be done!" One of the last thoughts of the dying man was to express the sentiment of his whole life, humility. Some one begged him to imitate the majority of the saints, who, on their death-bed, uttered a few pious words for the edification of their spiritual children. "They were saints," he replied, "and I am a sinner." A speech worthy of Saint Vincent de Paul, who, about to appear before God, replied to the person who requested his blessing, "It is not for me, unworthy wretch that I am, to bless you." The fervour with which he received the last sacraments aroused the admiration of all the witnesses of this supreme hour. They almost expected to see this holy soul take flight for its celestial mansion. As soon as the prayers for the dying had been pronounced, he asked to have the chaplets of the Holy Family recited, and during the recitation of this prayer he gave up his soul to his Creator. It was then half-past seven in the morning, and the sixth day of the month consecrated to the Holy Virgin, whom he had so loved (May, 1708).

It was with a quiver of grief which was felt in all hearts throughout the colony that men learned the fatal news. The banks of the great river repeated this great woe to the valleys; the sad certainty that the father of all had disappeared forever sowed desolation in the homes of the rich as well as in the thatched huts of the poor. A cry of pain, a deep sob arose from the bosom of Canada which would not be consoled, because its incomparable bishop was no more! Etienne de Citeaux said to his monks after the death of his holy predecessor: "Alberic is dead to our eyes, but he is not so to the eyes of God, and dead though he appear to us, he lives for us in the presence of the Lord; for it is peculiar to the saints that when they go to God through death, they bear their friends with them in their hearts to preserve them there forever." This is our dearest desire; the friends of the venerable prelate were and still are to-day his own Canadians: may he remain to the end of the ages our protector and intercessor with God!

There were attributed to Mgr. de Laval, according to Latour and Brother Houssart, and a witness who would have more weight, M. de Glandelet, a priest of the seminary of Quebec, whose account was unhappily lost, a great number of miraculous cures. Our purpose is not to narrate them; we have desired to repeat only the wonders of his life in order to offer a pattern and encouragement to all who walk in his steps, and in order to pay the debt of gratitude which we owe to the principal founder of the Catholic Church in our country.

The body of Mgr. de Laval lay in state for three days in the chapel of the seminary, and there was an immense concourse of the people about his mortuary bed, rather to invoke him than to pray for his soul. His countenance remained so beautiful that one would have thought him asleep; that imposing brow so often venerated in the ceremonies of the Church preserved all its majesty. But alas! that aristocratic hand, which had blessed so many generations, was no longer to raise the pastoral ring over the brows of bowing worshippers; that eloquent mouth which had for half a century preached the gospel was to open no more; those eyes with look so humble but so straightforward were closed forever! "He is regretted by all as if death had carried him off in the flower of his age," says a chronicle of the time, "it is because virtue does not grow old." The obsequies of the prelate were celebrated with a pomp still unfamiliar in the colony; the body, clad in the pontifical ornaments, was carried on the shoulders of priests through the different religious edifices of Quebec before being interred. All the churches of the country celebrated solemn services for the repose of the soul of the first Bishop of New France. Placed in a leaden coffin, the revered remains were sepulchred in the vaults of the cathedral, but the heart of Mgr. de Laval was piously kept in the chapel of the seminary, and later, in 1752, was transported into the new chapel of this house. The funeral orations were pronounced, which recalled with eloquence and talent the services rendered by the venerable deceased to the Church, to France and to Canada. One was delivered by M. de la Colombière, archdeacon and grand vicar of the diocese of Quebec; the other by M. de Belmont, grand vicar and superior of St. Sulpice at Montreal.

Those who had the good fortune to be present in the month of May, 1878, at the disinterment of the remains of the revered pontiff and at their removal to the chapel of the seminary where, according to his intentions, they repose to-day, will recall still with emotion the pomp which was displayed on this solemn occasion, and the fervent joy which was manifested among all classes of society. An imposing procession conveyed them, as at the time of the seminary obsequies, to the Ursulines; from the convent of the Ursulines to the Jesuit Fathers', next to the Congregation of St. Patrick, to the Hôtel-Dieu, and finally to the cathedral, where a solemn service was sung in the presence of the apostolic legate, Mgr. Conroy. The Bishop of Sherbrooke, M. Antoine Racine, pronounced the eulogy of the first prelate of the colony.

The remains of Mgr. de Laval rested then in peace under the choir of the chapel of the seminary behind the principal altar. On December 16th, 1901, the vault was opened by order of the commission entrusted by the Holy See with the conduct of the apostolic investigation into the virtues and miracles in specie of the founder of the Church in Canada. The revered remains, which were found in a perfect state of preservation, were replaced in three coffins, one of glass, the second of oak, and the third of lead, and lowered into the vault. The opening was closed by a brick wall, well cemented, concealed between two iron gates. There they rest until, if it please God to hear the prayers of the Catholic population of our country, they may be placed upon the altars. This examination of the remains of the venerable prelate was the last act in his apostolic ordeal, for we are aware with what precaution the Church surrounds herself and with what prudence she scrutinizes the most minute details before giving a decision in the matter of canonization. The documents in the case of Mgr. de Laval have been sent to the secretary of the Sacred Congregation of Rites at Rome; and from there will come to us, let us hope, the great news of the canonization of the first Bishop of New France.

Sleep your sleep, revered prelate, worthy son of crusaders and noble successor of the apostles. Long and laborious was your task, and you have well merited your repose beneath the flagstones of your seminary. Long will the sons of future generations go there to spell out your name,—the name of an admirable pastor, and, as the Church will tell us doubtless before long, of a saint.

The End

www.ingramcontent.com/pod-product-compliance
Lightning Source LLC
Chambersburg PA
CBHW070003300526
45794CB00001B/160